Peter Olsen Groth

A Danish and Dano-Norwegian grammar

Vol. 1

Peter Olsen Groth

A Danish and Dano-Norwegian grammar
Vol. 1

ISBN/EAN: 9783337724016

Printed in Europe, USA, Canada, Australia, Japan

Cover: Foto ©ninafisch / pixelio.de

More available books at **www.hansebooks.com**

Heath's Modern Language Series

A DANISH

AND

DANO-NORWEGIAN GRAMMAR

BY

...TH, A.M.

D. C. H...

COPYRIGHT, 1894
BY P. GROTH

ALL RIGHTS RESERVED

PRESS OF
𝕽ockwell and 𝕮hurchill
BOSTON, U.S.A.

PREFACE.

AS a teacher of the Danish or Norwegian language to English speaking students I had very often felt the lack of a reliable grammar of the language, and finally I made up my mind to try to supply the want. Special conditions of which I have not been master have caused the time intervening between the writing of this book and its appearance in print to be a good deal longer than it ought to have been, i. e. about two years, and meanwhile there have appeared a couple of Danish or Norwegian grammars that may deserve this name.

The reason why I have given my book the somewhat cumbersome title of a "Danish and Dano-Norwegian Grammar" will be apparent from the "Introduction." As regards the use of the book I would advise the student first to make up his mind, whether he wants to study the pure Danish language or the Dano-Norwegian language. This must to a large extent depend upon personal and practical considerations. The tourist, the commercial traveller, the merchant may need to study one branch of the language or the other; the literary student may wish to acquaint himself with genuine Danish, or he may wish to study the vernacular of Bjørnson and Ibsen. As a general rule I would say that the Danish pronunciation offers, with its "glottal catch" and other peculiarities, more difficulties to the English speaking student than the Norwegian pronunciation.

The student who wants to study D a n i s h must pass by §§ 81 to 146, while those who want to study N o r w e g i a n must pass directly from §§ 8 to 81. Besides, in the "Etymology," attention is often called to certain rules as being peculiar to Danish, others to Norwegian. The student must select those he needs, and pass by those that refer to the language that he is not studying.

I have added some "Exercises" at the end of the book in order to help the student fix in his memory those rules and paradigms which he must know before he can, with any degree of success, commence reading the language. For those who wish more exercises I can recommend Mr. K. BREKKE'S excellent *Lærebog i Engelsk* which is intended for Norwegian students of English, but may also to a certain extent be used the other way. The student may find an abundance of good r e a d e r s prepared for use in the Danish and Norwegian schools. I mention only Otto Borchsenius and F. Winkel Horn's *Dansk Læsebog*, Eriksen and Paulsen's *Norsk Læsebog*, Pauss and Lassen's *Læsebog i Modersmaalet*, each of them in several volumes. As Dictionaries can be thoroughly recommended: A. Larsen's *Dansk-Norsk Engelsk Ordbog* and Rosing's *Engelsk-Dansk Ordbog*. To those who want to study the Norwegian form of the language I would recommend: I. Brynildsen's *Norsk-engelsk ordbog* and the same author's edition of Geelmuyden's *Engelsk-norsk ordbog*. The tourist will find Bennett's *Phrasebook*, Olsvig's *Words and Phrases* and the same author's *Yes and No* valuable guides to familiarity with the peculiarities of the language.

This Grammar, besides being based upon my own studies and knowledge of the language, rests, as far as Danish is concerned, chiefly upon the works of *Sweet, Dahlerup and Jespersen, Jessen, Bojesen, Lefolii* and *B. T. Dahl*, and for the Norwegian upon the grammars of *Lökke* and *Hofgaard* and the treatises of *Storm, Western, Brekke* and *J. Aars*. To those who desire a more detailed knowledge of the language than can be had from this book I would recommend Poëstion's *Dänische Sprache* and the same author's *Lehrbuch der Norwegischen Sprache;* both these books are excellent, and especially the Danish Grammar has often been of use to me in writing this book.

The several species of types that are peculiar to the Scandinavian languages compelled me to have this book set in a Danish Newspaper printing office in New York City, not properly equipped for a work of this kind. On that account the typographical appearance of the book is not in every respect as good as I would like it to have been. Deserving of special mention is the fact that the types œ and æ are everywhere in the book used promiscuously to represent the latter character except in §92 where the sign œ is used a couple of times to denote and explain a variety of the sound of ö.

Finally I must acknowledge my debt of gratitude to Professor Dr. JOH. STORM of the University of Christiania for kindly sending me those advance sheets of the 2d edition of his "Englische Philologie" that were of use to me in preparing this grammar, to my honored friend Professor A. H. PALMER of Yale University for kindly reading through the larger part of the book in manuscript and making valuable suggestions, and, last but not least, to Mr. CHR. BØRS, late Consul of Norway and Sweden at New York, without whose munificience, proverbial among Norwegians in New York, this book would never have seen the light of day.

Brooklyn, N. Y., August 25th, 1894.

THE AUTHOR.

CONTENTS.

	Page.	Page.
INTRODUCTION..................................		1—2
THE ALPHABET.................................		3
DANISH SOUNDS..............................		4—29
Vowels.....................................	4	
Diphthongs	11	
Consonants................................	11	
Colloquial forms..........................	21	
Accent.....................................	21	
Sentence accent...........................	25	
Glottal Stop...............................	26	
Quantity...................................	28	
NORWEGIAN SOUNDS.........................		30—65
Vowels.....................................	30	
Diphthongs	35	
Consonants................................	36	
Accent.....................................	52	
Abbreviations	58	
Quantity...................................	63	
Vowel Changes in inflection and word formation......		66
Etymology......................................		67—131
Articles—genders..........................	67	
Nouns......................................	70—83	
Gender of the nouns....................	70	
Formation of the possessive............	76	
Syntactical remarks about the use of the possessive...	77	
Formation of the plural.................	78	

	Page.	Page.
The Adjectives.	83—91	
Declension of the adjectives.	83	
Use of the definite form of the adjectives.	86	
Agreement of the adjective with its noun.	87	
Comparison of adjectives.	87	
Inflection and use of the comparative and superlative.	90	
The Pronouns.	91—99	
The personal pronouns.	91	
The reflexive and reciprocal pronouns.	92	
The possessive pronouns.	93	
The demonstrative pronouns.	94	
The interrogative pronouns.	95	
The relative pronouns.	96	
The indefinite pronouns.	98	
The Numerals.	99—102	
The Verbs.	102—121	
Weak verbs.	104	
Strong verbs.	107	
Irregular verbs.	113	
The use of the numbers.	114	
The use of the tenses.	114	
The use of the modes.	116	
The passive voice.	119	
Reflexive and impersonal verbs	121	
The Adverbs.		122—124
The Prepositions.		124—1 6
The Conjunctions.		126—128
The Interjections.		128—129
The order of the words in the sentence.		129—130
The Punctuation		131
Exercises.		132—143

INTRODUCTION.

SCANDINAVIAN LANGUAGES. HISTORY OF THE DANO-NORWEGIAN LANGUAGE.

1. THE DANISH and DANO-NORWEGIAN language belongs to the SCANDINAVIAN group of the Teutonic languages. This group comprises, in modern times, besides the language already mentioned, the SWEDISH, NORWEGIAN, ICELANDIC and FAROISH languages.

2. The earliest specimens of Scandinavian language are found in the RUNIC inscriptions, written in the earlier Runic characters and dating as far back as the 4th century A. D. In these inscriptions the similarity with the other earlier specimens of Teutonic languages (especially Gothic) is more prominent than the peculiar Scandinavian characteristics.

3. During the VIKING AGE (750—1000 A. D.) the language of the Scandinavian nations underwent a very decided change. The Scandinavian peculiarities distinguishing the language from the other Teutonic idioms appear fully developed, and by and by dialectic differences between the languages of the several Scandinavian nations commence to assert themselves.

4. In the Middle Ages the Danish and Swedish languages form one group that may be designated as the EASTERN group of the Scandinavian languages, having in common the monophthongification of original diphthongs, while the Danish language had a development of its own in the direction of substituting voiced stops (mediae) or even open consonants (spirants) for voiceless stops (tenues, hard consonants) after a long vowel at the end of a word or syllable. The Norwegian language and its offspring the Icelandic tongue, on the other hand, form the WESTERN group of the Scandinavian languages, having in common the retention of the old diphthongs as diphthongs, but with some changes peculiar to each of the two languages. These two languages have, in common with the Swedish, retained the old voiceless stops.

5. In the Middle Ages we have the most valuable literature in the Norwegian-Icelandic language, consisting chiefly of the Eddic songs, the Scaldic art poetry, the Sagas and the Laws, while the chief products of the earliest Danish literature are the provincial laws and popular songs (folk lore), the latter not being reduced to writing until later.

6. When Norway in the latter part of the 14th century was united with Denmark, Norwegian literature fell into decay and Danish grew more and more to be the official language used in Court Documents, Royal Ordinances etc. In the latter part of the 17th century Norwegian authors again began to take an active part in the literature; but their language was Danish, this language having come to be adopted by the educated classes of the Norwegian people and chiefly by the inhabitants of the towns and cities, while the Norwegian language still remained the spoken idiom of most of the rural population. Still the language spoken and written by the educated classes in Norway was never pure Danish. Norwegian authors have always used some native words, taken from the rural dialects, in their writings, and while the official and professional people during the union with Denmark affected as far as possible a correct Danish pronunciation, the tendency in Norway now, even though it be unconscious, is to nationalize the language more and more. This tendency is chiefly noticeable in the pronunciation (retaining the voiceless stops, tenues), but it also appears in the grammar, especially the syntax, and in the vocabulary.

7. Thus it is that we have at the present time two kinds of Danish language, the pure Danish used in Denmark and by Danish authors, and the Dano-Norwegian used in Norway by most of the educated classes, especially in the cities, and by most of the Norwegian authors. Still it should be noted that the language spoken in Norway even by educated people is far more national in its character than the one used in writing.

THE ALPHABET.

8. The alphabet used in Danish and Dano-Norwegian literature has the same letters as the English alphabet and besides these the signs Æ (æ) and Ö (Ø, ø, ö). As for the sounds indicated by these letters see §§ 12, 13, 25, 26, 82, 91.

The names of the vowels are represented by their sounds.

The names of the consonants b, c, d, etc. are be, ce, de etc. (pronounce e like a in name.) h and k are called h a a and k a a (aa pron. with a sound between o in h o l e and a in call), j is called jod (yod), g ge (pronounced like g in give), w is called "dobbelt ve" (double v), z zet pr. set.

The Gothic characters are still in very common use, especially in newspapers and popular books. These letters have the following forms:

𝔄 a	𝔅 b	ℭ c	𝔇 d	𝔈 e	𝔉 f	𝔊 g	ℌ h	ℑ i	ℑ j
a	b	c	d	e	f	g	h	i	j
𝔎 k	𝔏 l	𝔐 m	𝔑 n	𝔒 o	𝔓 p	𝔔 q	𝔑 r	𝔖 s	
k	l	m	n	o	p	q	r	s	
𝔗 t	𝔘 u	𝔙 v	𝔚 w	𝔛 x	𝔜 y	ℨ z	𝔄𝔈 æ	𝔒 ö	
t	u	v	w	x	y	z	æ	ö	

Some authors also employ the sign å, borrowed from the Swedish language, to express the same sound as is usually in Danish and Dano-Norwegian literature denoted by a a (see above).

NOTE.—Capital letters are still according to official Danish rules of spelling used at the beginning of substantives and adjectives employed as substantives, while the official Norwegian orthography only acknowledges capital letters in proper nouns. A great many Danish authors also have done away with capital letters in common nouns.

The sounds of the Danish and the Dano-Norwegian branches of the language are so widely different, that it has been found practical to treat of them in separate chapters.

DANISH SOUNDS.

VOWELS.

9. Table of Danish vowels classified according to their articulation.

(A period· up in the line after a vowel indicates length of the vowel).

		BACK.		MIXED.		FRONT.	
		Not rounded.	Rounded.	Not rounded.	Rounded.	Not rounded.	Rounded
HIGH	Narrow		u·			i·	y·
	Wide		u			i	y
MID	Narrow		o·			e· e	ø ø·
	Wide		o	ə		æ	ö
LOW	Narrow		aa·			æ·	ö·
	Wide	a	aa				

[10. For the benefit of those not familiar with the phonetic terms as established by Mssrs. Bell, Sweet and others it is here remarked, that the terms "Back", "Mixed" and "Front" refer to the horizontal articulation of the tongue, indicating what part of the tongue has to be raised from its normal position in order to form such an articulation as to produce the vowel in question. Intermediate positions between those mentioned are designated by the names "advanced" or "outer" and "retracted" or "inner".

The words "High", "Mid" and "Low" refer to the vertical position of the tongue. An intermediate position between two of these positions may be described as a lowering of the position immediately above or a raising of the one below.

The terms "Narrow" and "Wide" refer to the shape of the tongue. "In forming "narrow" sounds there is a feeling of tenseness in that part of the tongue where the sound is formed, the surface of the tongue being made more convex than in its natural "wide" shape in which it is relaxed and flattened". (Sweet).

"Rounding is a contraction of the mouth cavity by lateral compression of the cheek passage and narrowing of the lip aperture" (Sweet).]

In Danish pronunciation of rounded vowels the rounding is accompanied by a projection of the lips so as to increase the length of the mouth cavity.

NOTE 1.—The articulation of Danish *a* is really advanced back, that of *e* raised mid. The vowels *aa* (å) and *o* are both pronounced with the same rounding as *o* and *u*, respectively, in common European pronunciation.

NOTE 2.—It should at once be noticed that in Danish pronunciation the lips play a more prominent part than in English, that the upper lip is never drawn so close to the teeth as in English pronunciation, and that the tongue normally has a more advanced and flattened position than with English speaking people.

SOUND VALUE OF DANISH VOWELS AND THEIR GRAPHIC REPRESENTATION IN COMMON ORTHOGRAPHY.

11. *A* has a sound very near that of English *a* in f a t h e r, although not quite as deep (somewhat palatalized). Ex. long: *Gade* street, *Abe* monkey; short: *Hat* hat, *Tak* thanks.

Note. The long *a* has in the vulgar Copenhagen pronunciation a sound very near English a in f a t prolonged   The foreigner must avoid imitating this pronunciation.

12. *æ* (long) has the same sound as English *ai* in a i r; Ex.: *Hær* army, *være* to be, *svæve* to hover.

This sound is in orthography represented by *e* in: *bedre* better, *der* there, *her* here, *deres* their, *ere* are, *regiere* to rule, *Regjering* government (and upond the whole before —*r*), *Legeme* body, *sjette* (pr. sjæte) sixth, *tjene* to serve, *fjer(d)e* fourth, *Stedet* the place, *udstede* to issue, *tilstede* to permit and other derivatives of *Sted; Chef* chief.

13. *œ* (short) has the same sound as English *e* in m e n; Ex.: *hæslig* ugly, *lægge* to lay.

This sound is in orthography as a rule represented by the sign *e* which is pronounced in this way in most cases when it is short and at the same time stressed; Ex.: *denne* this, *Ven* friend, *elske* to love, *Ende* end, *svensk* Swedish. It is written *æ* when derived from a word with long sound of *æ*, written *æ*, or from word with *a*, *aa* or *ei* in the root; Ex.: *kærlig* affectionate (from *kær* dear), *fælde* to fell (from *Fald* fall), *nægte* to deny (from *nej* no); *Hænder* hands (from *Haand* hand); furthermore in *Præst* priest and some other words.

14. *e* represents the sound of French é in é t é or of English *a* in n a m e, but without the diphthongic element of the latter (more like the common American pronunciation of *a*). This is the common sound of *e* when it is long (except before *r*, see § 12); Ex.: *se* to see, *Reb* rope, *Snes* score.

When a word in one form has a long *e*, then it, as a rule, retains the same quality of the sound, even if the vowel in other forms of the word is shortened: *hedt* hot (neuter of *hed*), *ledt* searched (partcp. of *lede*). The short variety of the same sound is also found in the unstressed prefixes *be*—and *ge*—: *bestemme* to decide; *Gemal* consort; furthermore in some monosyllables ending in —*d* or —*v*: *Bed* bed (in garden), *Fjed* step, *Drev* pinion (but *Sted* see § 12).

15. This sound (*e*) is represented by the orthographical sign of *i* in a great many cases where the vowel is short; especially is *i* pronounced this way before *mm*, *mp*, *nt*, *ng*, *nk*, besides some other cases; Ex.: *Fisk* fish (pron. fesk), *fiske* to fish, *ridse* to scratch, *Pligt* duty, *vil* will, *Spil* play, *Pille* pill, *digte* to make poetry, *lidt* a little (pron. let, but *lidt* suffered [partcp. of *lide*] pron lit), *midt* middle (pron. met, but *mit* mine pron. mit), *Skin* appearance, *Tin* tin, in the prefix *mis*, *misbruge* to misuse: *Misdæder* malefactor; unstressed in the derivative endings —*ling*,—*ning*: *Yndling* favorite, *Slægtning* relative. Some words may be spelt with either *i* or *e: tusinde* and *tusende* thousand,

Ærinde and Ærende errand (these two words may also be pronounced with *i*).

16. *ə* has a sound approaching that of French *e* in q u e, English *i* in b i r d. This sound only occurs in unaccented syllables, and its orthographic sign is *e*. Ex.: *Gave* gift, *Gade* street.

Some words may be pronounced and spelt with or without *ə* (e); Ex.: *tusind* and *tusinde* thousand, *hundred* and *hundrede* hundred, *Ærind* or *Ærinde* errand, *Billed(e)* picture, *Embed(e)* office, *Arbeid(e)* work, *Legem(e)* body, *Madam(e)*, *Himmerig(e)* kingdom of heaven, *Tind(e)* peak; in the words *Herre* Master, *Frue* Mistress, *Madame*, *Konge* king, *Fyrste* prince, *Greve* count the final *e* is omitted before a name or another title; *Herre* is then spelt *Hr.*: *Hr. Petersen* Mr. P.

17. Immediately after another stressed vowel *ə* is often slurred in the pronunciation, so as almost to disappear: *troəde* believed. In some cases it is written but not pronounced at all; it can never be pronounced immediately after a single vowel with glottal catch (see § 76) nor after a short stressed vowel. In some cases there may be a choice between a long stressed vowel with pronounced *ə* and a short vowel without *ə*. The former is then used in more select language, and especially is the retaining of *ə* common in the passive form; Ex.: *slaaes* to be beaten, but *slaas* to fight, *slaaet* and *slaa't* beaten, *gaaet* and *gaa't* gone. After *i* and *u e* is commonly retained (but *befri* liberate, *forny* renew, without *e* because of glottal catch).

An *e* is sometimes written without being pronounced, either to indicate length of the preceding vowel or to distinguish between different words of the same sound or words that although differing in sound would according to common rules have to be written in the same way. This *e* is called mute; Ex.: *saa(e)* saw, to distinguish it from *saa* so; *fo(e)r* (long o) went to distinguish from *for*, prp. for (short open å).

18. *i* has, when long (i·), about the same sound as English *ee* in s e e; Ex.: *Mine* mien, *Pibe* pipe, *smile* to smile.

When short it has the same sound as English *i* in f i l l; this sound occurs a) when the same word in another form or when the root word, from which the word in question is formed, has long i: *mit* my (neut. of min), *stri(d)t* fought, prtcp. of stride, *hvi(d)te* to whitewash, derived from *hvid* white; b) before *ld* or *lt*: *Sild* hering, *Milt* milt; c) in some other words; Ex.: *Kridt* chalk, *hid* here (hither), *Pisk* whip, *grisk* greedy; d) in unstressed syllables; Ex.: *Rival* rival, *imod* against.

The orthographic sign of this vowel is *i*, except in *de* they, *De* you, where it is e.

19. *aa* (å) has a sound similar to English *a* in c a l l, but closer. The long sound is as a rule written *aa*: *blaa* blue, *Naade* grace; but it is in some words denoted by *o* before v (except in diphthongs, see § 28) and *g*; Ex.: *Bog* book; *Brog* breeching, *broget* variegated, *klog* prudent, *koge* to cook, *Krog* hook, *kroget* crooked, *love* to promise, *Svoger* brother-in-law, *Drog* a good-for-nothing, *Fjog* booby, *Sprog* language, *Tog* expedition; unstressed in *Orlog* (naval) warfare, *Orlov* leave of absence (in the six last named words the vowel may be pronounced long and short); furthermore in *hvor* where, *Torsdag* Thursday, *borte* away, *Vorte* wart, *vore* ours, *otte* eight, (pron. å-te, but the ordinal *ottende* the eighth with short vowel), and unstressed *Alvor* earnest.

20. The short å-sound is as a rule denoted by the letter *o*; Ex.: *Lod* ½ ounce; *Boble* bubble, *Borg* castle, *hoppe* to jump, *Krop* body, *lokke* to allure, *vor* our.

The short sound of å is denoted by *aa* in some words formed by derivation or inflection of words with a long *aa*, and besides in some other words; Ex.: *blaat* blue (neut. of *blaa*), *vaadt* wet (neut. of vaad), *Skaansel* mercy (from *skaane* to treat with leniency), *Aadsel* corpse, *Aand* spirit, *Aande* breath, *Baand* ribbon, *Flaad* flux, *Haand* hand, *Laad* fleece, *laadden* fleecy, *en Maatte* a mat, *Raad* pus (but *Raad* council, long aa), *saa* so (when unstressed), *Saald* sieve (also written *Sold*), *Vaand* wand, *Vaande* jeopardy; and with secondary accent *Undersaat* a subject, *usaattes* on bad terms.

21. *O* is a sound peculiar to the Scandinavian languages, midway between English *o* in t o e and *oo* in t o o, but nearer the latter; and it is spoken with the same rounding of the lips as the English *oo*. The sound of *o* when long is in orthography represented by *o*, which letter when representing a long vowel generally denotes this sound; Ex.: *stor* large, *Blod* blood, *god* good, *Sko* shoe, *Bro* bridge (as for o with sound of long å see § 19).

22. The short sound of *o* is represented in orthography by *o* in the following cases: 1) in words formed by inflection, derivation or composition from a root word or form with long *o*; Ex.: *nordisk* Northern (from *nor(d)*, *Gods* goods (from *god* good), (but *godt* neuter of *god*, pron. gåt); 2) in unstressed first syllables before a single consonant: *Hotel*, *Koloni*, *brodere* to embroider (also in *Hospital*, *Osteri*); 3) in the following words: *Kost* broom, *ond* bad, *Onsdag* Wednesday, *Ost* cheese, *sort* black, *Torden* thunder.

23. Otherwise the short sound of *o* is represented in common orthography by *u*, which sign when representing a short vowel usually indicates this sound (except in the cases stated in § 24); Ex.: *Dug* dew (but *Dug* table cloth with u·); *smuk* nice, *Buk* he-goat, *lukke* close, *slukke* extinguish, *Hul* hole, *dum* foolish, *stum* mute, *Hummer* lobster; unstressed in *fordum* formerly. Some words may be spelt with either *u* or *o*, the pronunciation in both cases being o; Ex.: *Kunst* and *Konst* art, *Kummen* and *Kommen* caraway, *Kuffert* and *Koffert* traveller's trunk.

24. *u* represents a sound similar to the English *oo*, but closer; Ex.: *Hus* house, *bruge* to use, *ud* out. A short sound of *u*, similar to English *u* in full, occurs in some cases: 1) in words derived from words or forms with long *u* or *y*; Ex.: *brugt* partc. of *bruge* to use, *skudt* partc. of *skyde* to shoot; 2) in unstressed syllables; Ex.: *ugjörlig* impossible, *Musik*, *Uniform*; 3) when *u* is followed by *ld*, *lt* or *sk*; Ex.: *fuld* full, *Guld* gold, *sulte* to starve, *fuske* to bungle; 4) in the words: *Krudt* gunpowder, *Lut* lute, *lurvet* shabby, and some others (about *u* in other cases representing the sound of *o* see § 23).

25. ø has a sound like French *eu* in *peu*; the English language has no corresponding sound (to produce the sound one should say *a* as in English f a t e and at the same time hold the lips in almost the whistling position); Ex.: *Födsel* birth, *Bønder* peasants, *Søster* sister, *Stød* blow, *høre* to hear, *lød* sounded (impf. of *lyde*), *Sølv* silver, *løs* loose, *Prøve* trial, *Bøger* books. The sound of ø is represented by the letter ø (ö) always when it is long, and sometimes when short. But the short sound of ø is as a rule in writing represented by the sign of *y*; Ex.: *Tryk* pressure, *Stykke* piece, *dryppe* to drip, *dyrke* to cultivate, *Fyrste* a prince, *kysse* to kiss, *Lygte* lantern, *Lykke* fortune, *Nytte* utility, *skylle* to rinse, *synke* to sink.

26. ö has a more open sound, like French *eu* in p e u p l e, German ö. (Pronounce English *a* in f a t with the lips in a whistling position); Ex.: *förste* first, *Berömmelse* fame, *större* larger, *Björn* bear, *Bönner* prayers, *Sön* son, *forsömme* to neglect.

NOTE. In Danish spelling there is not as a rule made a consistent distinction between the signs ö and ø, most writers using both signs promiscuously or either one exclusively.*) ö is as a rule used before *m*, *n* ending a word, *nn*, *rr*, *rn*. (As for the sound and use of ö as first part of a diphthong see § 28).

27. *y* has the sound of French u, German ü; the English language has no corresponding sound (to produce it the tongue takes the position for *i*, the lips that for *u*). The letter y represents this sound 1) when it is long; Ex.: *flyde* to flow, *adlyde* to obey, *sy* to sew, *Öjenbryn* eyebrow, *Tyv* thief, *Sky* cloud; 2) when short, a) in case the root word or form has long *y*; Ex.: *dybt* neuter af *dyb* deep, *nyt* neuter af *ny* new; b) in unstressed syllables; Ex.: *Hypothék* mortgage, *Hyperbol*,

---

*) As for consistency in pronunciation the Danish grammarian Dr. Jessen says, that it is not easy to find two persons who agree on this point.

Fysik; c) when *y* is followed by the combinations *ld* or *lt;* Ex.: *fylde* to fill, *Stylte* stilt; d) in some other words; Ex.: *Frygt* fright, *styg* ugly, *tyk* thick. (As for the letter y representing the sound of ø see § 25.)

DANISH DIPHTHONGS.

28. Danish spelling has the following Diphthongs:
av, ov, æv, öv and *aj, ej, oj, öj*.

The consonant part of these diphthongs has in spite of the peculiar Danish spelling with *v* and *j* the sounds of *w* and *i**). In the diphthongs of the w-series the vowel part retains its peculiar sound (*a, o, æ, ö*); Ex.: *Havn* harbor, *hævne* to revenge, *nævne* to name, *hovne* to swell, *Hövl* plane, *Stövle* boot, *Vrövl* nonsense; but in the i-series *a* and *e* are pronounced as *a, o* and *ö* as a sound approaching *å*; *aj* and *ej* are pronounced like English *y* in my, *oj* and *öj* like English *oy* in boy; *vaje* to wave and *veje* to weigh pronounced in the same manner; *böje* to bend and *Boje* a buoy, both pronounced alike. Another sign for the diphthong *ej* is *eg;* Ex.: *jeg* pr. jaj; *Vegne* in *allevegne*, everywhere (pron. vainə, e. g. rhyme: *Vegne, Hygiajne*). 16 is now spelt *sejsten*, formerly *sexten*. *Nögle* (pr. nåilə) key; *Vindbeutel* (pron. venbåitl) braggart; but in *Zeus, Europa* etc. *eu* is pronounced *öv*.

DANISH CONSONANTS.

29. The difference between tenues (p, t, k) and mediae (b, d, g) is not so much dependent upon the circumstance of

---
*) Some Danish grammarians think that the Danish diphthongs really have the consonants v and j for their second part.

the former being voiceless, the latter voiced, as is the case in English. But the Danish tenues are followed by a voiceless breath, thereby becoming aspirates. Thus the energy of expiration becomes the chief distinguishing feature between Danish tenues and mediae.

In some cases the tenues are written where the sound is really nearer to that of the mediae; thus *Nordens Skuder* (the ships of the North) and *Nordens Guder* (the gods of the North) are both pronounced in almost the same manner (*sguder*), i. e. the aspiration of tenues does not take place after *s* and thus the chief characteristic of the hard sound disappears. The same rule applies to shut consonants written double in the middle of words, *pp*, *tt*, *kk* representing about the same sound as *bb*, *dd*, *gg*; Ex.: *tykke* thick, plur., and *tygge* to chew, *Bække* rivulets, and *begge* both, *Lapper* patches, and *Labber* paws, have the same sound, something between tenues and mediae.

30. *p* has the hard aspirated sound of p-h (not ph=f) in the beginning of syllables: *Pære* pear, *Penge* money, *Parade*.

The sound of *p* is written *b* before *s* and terminative *t* (*te*), the long root vowel at the same time being shortened; Ex.: *Ribs* currants, *Stribs* flogging, *dybt* deep (neut. of *dyb*), *dræbte* killed, impf. of *dræbe*, *tabt* lost, partcp. of *tabe* to lose.

31. 1) After s, 2) when written double (*pp*) and 3) at the end of words the sign *p* represents the sound midway between *p* and *b*, or a hard *b*; Ex.: *spare* to save (sb), *pippe* to peep up (pron. p-hibbə), *op* up, pron. obb (bb in these cases indicating the hard sound of b).

32. In some foreign words *ph* indicates the sound of *f* (see § 36). *Pharisæer*, *Philosophi* (more commonly now spelt with f). In *Ps* in Greek words p is mute: *Psalme* psalm (also written *Salme*); in others like *Psykologi* psychology, *Psalter*, *Pseudonym*, *Ptolemæus* it is sounded by some people, omitted by others.

33. *b* is pronounced as the voiced labial stop (Engl. b) 1) in the beginning of a word or a syllable; Ex.: *bade* to bathe, *Brok* hernia, *Blæk* ink, *Taabe* fool; 2) at the end of a word or a syllable after a l o n g vowel; Ex.: *Gab* gap, *Stab* stoff, *Daab* baptism.

34. The sound midway between *b* and *p* is represented by the sign of *b*, 1) at the end of a word or syllable after a short vowel; Ex.: *Lab* paw, *Grib* vulture; 2) when written double between two vowels: *Labber* paws, *Ribbe* rib.

35. *m* like English m: *Mad* food, *ham* him; double *m* (mm) pronounced short: *kom(m)e* to come.

36. *f* is a labiodental voiceless open consonant and has a sound similar to English f: *faa* few, *Skuffe* drawer, *Ruf* deckhouse.

In some words the sound of *f* is represented in writing by *v*: thus in the beginning of the foreign words: *Vernis* varnish, *Viol*, violet, *Violin*, and also sometimes before t as in *grovt* rough (neut. of *grov*), *havt* had (prtcp. of *have*) pron. *groft*, *haft*, which now also is the official way of spelling.

NOTE. *Stiffader* stepfather, pronounced *stefar*, so also other compounds with *stif-* step- pronounced ste.

37. *v* is a labiodental open voiced consonant similar in pronunciation to English v; it occurs in the beginning of words and after a consonant, after a long vowel and in foreign words; Ex.: *Van(d)* water, *Sværd* sword, *evig* eternal, *lavt* low (neuter), *Avis* newspaper.

In the pronunciation of the Copenhagen dialect *v* often takes the place of *b* after a vowel; *løbe* pron. *løve*, *Köbenhavn* pron. *Kövenhavn*; in some words both forms are written promiscuously: *Knebel* and *Knevel*, *knevle* and *knebls* gag and to gag.

The sound of *v* is written *f* in *af* præp. of, pron. *av*, *aw* (see § 28), *a*.

38. For *v* being the sign of the w-sound in diphthongs, see § 28. Some words may be pronounced both with diphthong (the vowel preceding *v* then being short) and with a long vowel and *v*; Ex.: *Hav* sea pron. Ha·v or Haw, *Skove* forests pron. Skå·ve or Skåwe, *over* over, pron. å·ver or åwer. The vowels *a* and *o* are mostly short before *v* (implying the diphthongic pronunciation), but there are some exceptions: *bra·v* brave, *Gra·v* grave, *Kra·v* claim, *la·v* low, *ga·v* gave (impf. of give), *gro·v* dug (impf. af grave).

39. Colloquially *v* is often dropped after *l*: *hal(v)* half, *tol(v)* 12, *søl(v)* silver; after a long vowel: *bra(v)* brave, *ga(v)* gave, *gi(v)* give, *bli(v)* become, *ble(v)* became. Between two vowels, the second of which is ə, *v* is often dropped together with the following ə; Ex.: *ha(ve)* to have, *gi(ve)* to give, *gi(ve)r* gives, *bli(ve)r* becomes, *Hoved* head, pron. Hoðə in its original meaning, but Hoveð in compound words used figuratively: *Hovedsag* matter af chief importance, *Hovedstad* capital, *ha(ve)* to have, imperf. pron. haðe written *havde*.

40. *t* an aspirated English t (t-h, but not an open (spirantic) sound like English th); Ex.: *Tag* roof, *ti* ten. After *s* the aspiration does not take place, so *st* sounds almost like *sd*: *Sted* place, pron. *Sdeð*. Also *tt* sounds almost like a *d*, but without voice: *mætte* satisfied (plur.), pron. mæ'də (see § 29).

41. The sound of *t* is in Danish spelling in some words rendered by *th* in conformity with the old pronunciation; Ex.: *thi* (conjunction) for; *Thing* diet (to distinguish it in writing from *Ting* thing). Also in words of Greek origin: *Theater*, *Throne*, *Theori*.

42. *t* is at the end of the unstressed syllable in words of two syllables or more pronounced as a soft ð (see § 46); especially in participles and words with the definite article; Ex.: *böjet* bent (bojeð), *Huset* (ð) the house. But in foreign words with the stress upon the second syllable *t* is pronounced as t: *Serviet* napkin.

43. *t* is written but not pronounced in adverbs ending in *igt*; Ex.: *tydeli(gt)* plainly; in the article and pronoun *de(t)*.

44. In foreign words *ti* before a vowel as a rule is pronounced as *tsi*; Ex.: *partiel, Kvotient, Differentiering* differentiation; but the ending t i o n is pronounced as sjon: *Nation* pron. Nasjon, *Motion* exercise, pron. Mosjon.

45. *d* has a sound like English *d*, but less voiced, 1) in the beginning of words: *Dal* valley, *Dok* dock, *din* thine; 2) in the middle and at the end of words after a consonant (if not mute (see § 47); Ex.: *Olding* old man, *Forældre* parents, *Byrd* birth, *lærd* learned; 3) between two vowels, when the word is of foreign origin or a proper noun: *Soda, Adam, Edda*.

46. The sign *d* also represents an o p e n consonant with a sound similar to that of English soft *th* in f a t h e r; in pronouncing this "soft" d (phonetic sign ð) the tip of the tongue is allowed to remain in the lower part of the mouth, while the front of the tongue is raised towards the gums and the breath is gently squeezed between the tongue and the gums. This sound occurs:

1) in the middle of words between two vowels (also when written double: *Padde* toad, *Kladde* rough-draught; but *Bredde* breadth and *Vidde* width, have closed *d*); Ex.: *bede* to beg, *græde* to cry, weep, *Naade* grace, *Maade* manner; 2) in the middle of words after a vowel before j, l, m, n, r and the genitive *s*; Ex,: *dadle* to reproach, *Sedler* bills, *rödme* to blush, *krydre* to spice; 3) at the end of a word after a vowel; Ex.: *Gud* God, *Stud* bullock, *Vid* wit. Also when ending the first part of a compound word, even if the second part begins with a hard consonant; Ex.: *Blodtab* loss of blood, *udsat* exposed.

47. *d* is written but not pronounced (mute) 1) in most cases after *l* and *n*; Ex.: *Gul(d)* gold, *Il(d)* fire, *smæl(d)e* to crack (a whip), *Skul(d)er* shoulder, *hol(d)e* to hold, *Haan(d)* hand, *Venin(d)e* lady friend.

NOTE. *d* is pronounced after *l* and *n* a) in derivative adjectives ending in —ig and —elig; Ex.: *mandig* manful, *sandelig* truthfully; b) when followed by *r*; Ex.: *forandre* to change, *hindre* to prohibit, *Forældre* parents; c) in the ending —ende; Ex.: *læsende* reading, *Tidende* news; d) in some specific words: *Olding* old man, *Ælde* age, *Vælde* power, *Bande* gang, *Blonde* lace, *Grande* neighbor, *Kunde* customer; and in foreign words: *Indien* East India, *Cylinder*, *Gelænder* bannisters. (*Ynde* grace, charm, pron. Önde, but *ynde* to favor, pron. önne).

2) After *r* when the preceding vowel is long; Ex.: *Bord* table (pron. *Bor*), *Or(d)* word, *Jor(d)* earth (sometimes on the pulpit and in similar style pronounced *Jord* with short o and audible d); *jor(d)et* earthy, without d, *jordet* buried, with d. But when the preceding vowel is short *d* is pronounced after *r*: *Færd* voyage, and *færdes* to travel, (but *paafær(d)e* abroad, afoot), *Byrd* birth, *Byrde* burden.

NOTE. In *nordisk* northern, the *d* is pronounced but in *Norden* it is not unless when signifying the three Scandinavian countries; *nor(d)enfor* to the north of, *nor(d)enfra* from the north etc.

3) Before an —s (not being the genitive ending) *d* as a rule is not pronounced (and it is never pronounced before *sk* or between *n* and *s*); *be(d)st* best, *Lo(d)s* pilot, *en Stads* of a city (gen.), but *Sta(d)s* state, show. In compound words the —s as a rule originally is the genitive ending and therefore the *d* is pronounced; Ex.: *Daadskraft* energy, but *Baa(d)smand* boatswain, *Baa(d)shage* boat-hook; in adverbs which originally are genitive forms *d* is pronounced: *allesteds* etc., everywhere; in *tilfreds* satisfied *d* may be pronounced or not.

4) Before *t*: *go(d)t* neuter of *god* good, *spæ(d)t* neuter of *spæd* tender, *et Ri(d)t* a ride.

5) Before *k* in the words *Bø(d)ker* cooper, *Sne(d)ker* joiner.

48. In many words of frequent occurrence *d* between two vowels is dropped together with the following vowel when the latter is ǝ; such words are *Fader*, *Moder*, *Broder* pron. *Far*, *Mor*, *Bror* father, mother, brother; in compounds also written in the short form: *Farfader* father's father, but *Fadermorder* parricide, *Mormor* mother's mother, *Fjeder* or *Fjer* feather, *Foder* or *Foer* pron. for, fodder or lining (generally spelt with d in the former meaning without it in the latter); *Spar* or *Spa(de)r* spades (in cards) but *Spader* (spaðər) spades (as a tool); *han la(de)r* he lets (præs. of *la(de)* to let), *Klæ(de)r* clothes, but *Klæder* cloths (generally called *Sorter Klæde* kinds of cloth), *Læ(de)r* leather. *d* is also in common conversation dropped at the end of many words of common occurrence: *go(d)* good, *han lo(d)* he let, *sto(d)* stood, *ve(d)* with, *jeg ve(d)* I know, *(h)va(d)* what; also *Kjedel* kettle, pron. *Kele*.

This dropping of the *d* may be used as a means of distinguishing two meanings of one word; thus *vid* wide is pronounced *vi* when signifying wide in opposition to narrow: *et Par vi(d)e Buxer* a pair of wide trousers; but *uden videre* without further (ado), *og saavidere* etc., *den vide Verden* the wide, wide world.

49. *n* has the same sound as in English; *ng* has the same sound as English ng in s i n g e r; Ex.: *Finger* finger, *Sanger* singer; the same sound is before *k* represented by *n* alone; so also in some foreign words before *g*; Ex.: *sanke* (pron. sangke) to gather, *Enke* (ngk) widow, *Evangelium* (ngg) gospel, *Ungarn* (ngg) Hungary.

50. *l* has the same sound as in English.

51. *s* never has the soft (voiced) sound of English s between vowels. Ex.: *Hus* house, *sy* to sew (s in both cases pronounced alike). *sj* represents one single sound, that of a palatalized *s*, similar in sound to English *sh*; Ex.: *sjelden* seldom, *Sjæl* soul.

German *sch*, English *sh*, French *ch*, *g*, *j* are by the Danes pronounced with this same sound in words borrowed from those languages: *Schak* chess, *Shavl* shawl, *Choc* onset, *Chocolade*, *jaloux* (sj.) *genere* (sj.) to worry.

52. *j* is a palatal open voiced (except after k, p, t) consonant corresponding in sound to English *y* before vowels; Ex.: *ja* yes, *jeg* (pron. jai) I.

For j representing the sound of *i* in the second part of diphthongs see § 28.

j is often written without being pronounced after *k* and *g* before *æ*, *ö* and open *e*. *K(j)ær* dear, *g(j)erne* willingly. (According to the latest official rules of spelling this *j* is not to be written except in Danish names such as *Kjøge*, *Kjøbenhavn*, where the use of j is optional). Before other vowels than those mentioned *j* is pronounced (except in the Copenhagen dialect); *Kjole* dress coat, woman's gown; *gjor(d)e* did.

53. *k* is an aspirated tenuis; *kalde* pron. k-hal.ɔ; the aspiration does not take place after *s* and when written double in the middle of words, see § 29. *Ikke* not, forming rhyme with *ligge*, *Sukke* sighs (plur.) forming rhyme with *Vugge* cradle, *skal* shall, pron. sgal.

54. *g* is not so distinctly voiced as the corresponding English sound, to which it otherwise corresponds. *g* occurs 1) in the beginning of words; Ex.: *Gave* gift, *grave* to dig, *glide* to slide, *give* to give; 2) in the middle of words a) when written double: *ligge* to lie, *begge* both; b) between two vowels in foreign words: *Agurk* cucumber, *Cigar*; 3) in the end af words after a short vowel: *styg* ugly, *Byg* barley, *Hug* cut, blow; sometimes after a long vowel: *Æg* egg, definite form *Ægget*, where the double g (gg) is the sign of this sound and does not indicate the shortness of the preceding vowel.

55. The sign of *g* also represents an open (spirantic) guttural voiced sound, similar to German g in l e g e n, T a g e. This sound never occurs in the beginning of words, but 1) in the middle of words between two vowels (but not after a short æ or ö), or between a vowel and a voice consonant or two voice consonants; 2) at the end of words after a long vowel or a voice consonant; Ex.: *bage* to bake, *vige* to yield, *sluge* to devour, *kogle* to charm, *vaagne* to awaken, *Mængde* quantity.

NOTE 1. For *g* serving as orthographical sign of the sound *i* in diphthongs see § 28.

g represents this sound 1) after the vowels open *e* or *ö* before *l* or *n* or before a termination commencing with unstressed ə; 2) in the end of words after a short open *e*, *æ* or *ö*; Ex.: *Nögle* (öj) key, *Egn* (aj) region, *jeg* (aj) I, *Leg* (aj) play, *meget* (ajɔt) much, *legede* (ajə) played; 3) in the pronouns *mig* me, *dig* thee, you, *sig* him (her) self (pron. *maj* etc.). (Colloquially these pronouns are when unstressed pronounced jə, mə, də, sɔ, and in church oratory and recitations the three last mentioned may be pronounced as written *mig*, *dig*, *sig*, but that is never the case with *jeg*). In stead of *dejg* dough, *feig* cowardly, *sejg* tough the official orthography now is *dej*, *fej*, *sej*.

NOTE 2. *g* serves as the sign of the sound *w* in diphthongs (see § 28) after the sound å written o) in: *Rogn* spawn, *Sogn* parish, *Vogn* wagon. (In stead of the former spelling, *Laug* guild, *Sang* saw, *taug* was silent, *Ploug* plough, *Toug* rope, there is now generally written *Lav*, *Sav*, *tav*, *Plov*, *Tov*. Wholly antiquated is the spelling *Hauge* for *Have* garden).

56. In common every day pronunciation *g* is often dropped: 1) after long *u* in *slu(g)e* to devour, *su(g)e* to suck, *Ku(g)le* bullet, *Fu(g)l* fowl, (the g was in these cases first assimilated to *u* and then dropped); 2) after long *i* in: *li(g)e* straight, direct, *Pi(g)e* girl, *si(g)e* to say, *Skri(g)* cry etc. (g in these cases was assimilated to j and then dropped); 3) after *l* and *r*: *sæl(g)e* to sell; *spör(g)e* to ask; impf. *sol(g)te* sold, *spur(g)te* (sporte) asked, *dul(g)te* concealed; 4) In *ta(ge)r* takes, *ta(ge)* to take, *to(g)* took, *slo(g)* struck, *la(gde)* laid.

57. The *r* commonly used by educated Danes is the untrilled back or throat r, produced by raising the back of the tongue towards the roof of the pharynx; this *r* is as a rule voiced, but it is voiceless after aspirated stops; it is never vocalic like English final *r*; Ex.: *Raab* cry, *træt* tired, (*han*) *løber* he runs.

NOTE. In Jutland and in some other local dialects the *r* is pronounced with a strong trill, either front or uvular; the latter pronunciation is especially employed in the stage and pulpit language.

R is dropped in the pronunciation of the appellative noun: *Ka(r)l* a man, laborer (in the derivative *Kælling*, an old woman, *r* is not even retained in writing), but in the proper noun *Karl* Charles, *r* retains its sound.

58. *h* has the same sound as English h; it is pronounced before vowels in the beginning of a word or a syllable; Ex.: *han* he, *udholde* to endure, *Mæhæ* ninny.

NOTE 1. In some words *h* is written before j and *v* without influencing the pronunciation: (*H*)*vile* rest, (*H*)*jul* wheel.

NOTE 2. A vowel ending a sentence is in Danish pronounced with a peculiar breath that may be compared with an *h*. This is not indicated in spelling; *vi* we, pron. (in the position mentioned) vih, *nu* now, pron. nuh.

59. *C* only occurs in foreign words and is pronounced as *s* and *k* according to the same rules as in English; Ex.: *Centrum, Scene, Accent*.

According to the latest official orthography *c* is only to be used indicating the sound of *k* before an other *c* that represents the sound of *c*; in all other cases it is to be replaced by k: *Vokal, Konsonant*.

60. *ch* is in words of Greek origin pronounced as k and now also officially written that way; it indicates the same sound in the proper names *Tycho* and *Munch*, but in words of French origin *ch* is usually pronounced as *sj*: *Chaussé* highway. *sch* in words of German origin is pronounced like Danish sj. Instead of a former *sch* (*ch*) there is now in many words regularly written *sk*: *Droske* cab, *Mansket* cuff, *Marskal, Marskandiser* fripper, *Skak* chess, *Skatol* cabinet, *Skak* shaft, *Skallottelög* eschalot.

61. *Q* only occurs before *v* in foreign words, but it is now mostly in those of such words as are in popular use replaced by *k*. *Kvinde* woman is now only by very oldfashioned people spelt *Quinde*; *Kvartét, Kvint*.

62. *W* only occurs in foreign words and has the sound of v. *Wien* Vienna.

63. *X* according to the latest rules is to be replaced by *ks* in words of common use: *seks* six, *Okse* ox.

64. *Z* represents the sound of *s* and is only used in foreign words. In words of German origin it is to be replaced by *s: sitre* to tremble, *sire* to adorn; in other foreign words it is to be retained: *Zone, Zenit, Zelot*.

COLLOQUIAL FORMS.

65. In colloquial language words of frequent occurrence and of no particular logical importance undergo some abbreviations and changes besides those already spoken of. Some of the most important of them may here be mentioned.

at, to, before infinitives pronounced å.

den is enclitically pronounced 'n: *gi me'n* for *giv mig den* give it me.

det (which proclitically is pronounced *de:* *de(t) store Hus* the big house) is enclitically pronounced 'ð: *si me'ð* for *sig mig det* tell it me.

endnu yet, pron. inu.

idet when, pron. ide' (see § 43).

nej no, pron. næ.

og and, pron. å (thus taking the same form as the infinitive particle *at*, with which it is often confounded).

ogsaa also, pron. o'så.

skal shall pron. sga.

til to, pron. t-he.

tredive 30, pron. treðvə.

vil will, pron. ve.

DANISH ACCENT.

66. The accent stress in Danish as a rule rests on the root-syllable, which in most cases is the first syllable. The accent stress is not in common writing indicated by any orthopraphic sign.

67. Some derivative suffixes take the accent: —*ads*, —*inde*, —*i*; Ex.: *Mora'ds* morass, *Veni'nde* lady friend, *Værdi'* value.

68. Foreign words as a rule have the accent on the same syllable as in the language from which they have been adopted: *Stude'nt, Korpora'l, Universite't, Fami'lie, Ame'rika*.

Note 1. In a few foreign words the accent is on another syllable than in the language from which they were taken; Ex.: *Talle'rken* dish plate, from Low G. *Te'llerken;* *Bersœ'rk* from O. N. *be'rserkr;* *Valky'rie* from O. N. *va'lkyria*.

Note 2. In words ending in —*or* (adopted from the Latin) the accent in plural moves according to the Latin rule: *Profe'ssor, Professo'rer* (but with the definite article *Profe'ssoren* the professor).

69. Adjectives derived in —*agtig* and —*haftig* (German endings) have the accent on the termination: *barna'gtig* childish, *dela'gtig* partaking, *mandha'ftig* mannish; the same is also the case with most adjectives ending in —*isk: parti'sk* partial; *poli'sk* sly (but *kri'gerisk* warlike).

The ending —*lig* often has the power of moving the accent towards the ending of the word: *sædva'nlig* customary (but *Sæ'dvane* custom), *eventy'rlig* marvellous (but *E'ventyr* adventure).

70. In c o m p o u n d words the first part as a rule takes the c h i e f a c c e n t ('), the first syllable of the second part a s e c o n d a r y a c c e n t ('); Ex.: *Hu'slæ'rer* private tutor, *Prø'veaa'r* trial year; *Blo'msterpo'tte* flower pot.

71. The chief accent is on the second part of compound words. a) in substantives; 1) in some Scandinavian local names: *Kø'benha'vn* Copenhagen, *Ko'rsø'r;* 2) in some compounds, where the second part qualifies the first part: *Aarhu'ndrede* century, *Aartu'sinde* millennium, *Aarti'* decennium (but *Fe'maar* lustrum); 3) in some titles: *Borgme'ster* burgomaster, *Generallö'jtnant* lieutenant general; 4) in the words: *nordo'st* northeast, *nordve'st* northwest etc., and in *Skjærso'mmer* month of June, *Pebermy'nte* peppermint, *Skarnty'de* hemlock, *Fastela'vn* shrovetide, *Skjærto'rsdag* Maundy Thursday, *Langfre'dag* Good Friday; 5) in words, the second part of which is *lille*: *Barnli'lle* little child, *Morli'lle* dear mother; 6) in some words the first part of which is a verbal stem, the second an adverb: *Paso'p* (dog's name), *Farve'l* farewell; b) in adjectives:

1) in some adjective derivatives in *-ig* or *-lig*: *agtvæ'rdig* estimable, *tilbø'rlig* proper, *hævngje'rrig* vindictive, *frimo'dig* frank, *taalmo'dig* patient (but *ho'vmodig* haughty), *nederdræ'gtig* mean. But most compound adjectives formed in this manner have the accent on the first part of the composition: *ski'nhellig* hypocritical, *ma'ngesidig* manysided, *e'nsformig* uniform; no strict rules can be given, because the language of different persons differs even in the same words, and sometimes similar words differ without any apparent reason (Ex.: *ko'rtvarig* of short duration; but: *langva'rig* of long duration) and in some cases difference in accent serves to indicate difference of meaning; Ex.: *enfo'ldig* simple minded, *e'nfoldig* yielding a return equal to the seed sown; 2) in adjectives derived in *-som* and *-bar*: *opfi'ndsom* inventive, *udfø'rbar* practicable; 3) in compound adjectives the first part of which is *al*: *alvi'dende* omniscient, *almæ'gtig* almighty, *ale'ne* alone; 4) in some other compound adjectives: *höjvelbaa'ren* nobel, *höjæ'del* highly noble, *höjstæ'ret* highly honored, *medli'dende* sympathetic, *tilfre'ds* satisfied;

c) compound adverbs the first part of which is *der* or *her* and the second part a preposition, are accentuated on the first part, if they commence the sentence; if not, they are accentuated according to the logical importance of the component parts (see § 75): *de'ri har De Ret* there you are right, *han gik derfra' med tungt Hjerte* he left (literally: went thence) with a heavy heart; *e'ngang* once (but no more), *enga'ng* once upon a time; *desvæ'rre* alass, *desu'den* besides (but *de'sforuden* besides), *desli'ge* in the same manner, *de'suagtet* never the less, *de'sangaaende* thereabout; also adverbs compound with *saa-* and *hvor-* change accent according to the logical importance of the component parts: *saasna'rt* (*som*) as soon as (but *saa'snart* so soon), *saa'meget* so much, *saamœ'nd* indeed, *saavi'dt* as far as (but *saa'ledes* thus, *saa'som* because), *hvornaa'r* when, *hvorle'des* how (but *hvo'rledes* in what manner), *hvorda'n* how, *hvorve'l* albeit, *hvorvi'dt* whether. Compound adverbs consisting of a preposition with a following substantive or adjective used as substantive as a rule have the accent on the second part; Ex.: *igæ're* going on, *afste'd* off, *overa'lt* everywhere, *itu'* a sunder, *eflerhaa'nden* by and by, *oversty'r* to naught, (*komme*) *overe'ns* (to come) to terms, *foru'den* outside of, *foro'ven* above, *forne'den* below, *tilsa'mmen* together. (But *o'verhaands*, *o'vervættes* exceedingly, *a'fsides* apart, *fo'rlods* in advance). Furthermore may be noted: *alde'les* wholly, *fremde'les* further, *særde'l°s* especially, *allere'de* already, *alli'gevel* though, *maaske'*, *kanske'* perhaps, *monstro'* I wonder.

72. In words compound with the (originally German) prefixes *be-*, *er-*, *for-*, *ge-* the accent as a rule is on the syllable following next to the prefix; Ex.: *begri'be* to understand, *erfa're* to learn, *Forsta'nd* sense, *Gehø'r* (musical) ear. The originally German prefix *for* (Ger. ver) is to be distinguished from the originally Danish prefix of the same sound corresponding to English f o r e in such words as *Fo'rmiddag* forenoon, *Fo'rløber* forerunner.

73. The Danish prefix *u-*, Eng un-, takes the accent except in adjectives derived (chiefly from verbs) with the terminations -*lig*, -*elig*, -*bar*, -*som*. *U'ro* disquiet, *U'aar* bad year, *uska'delig* harmless, *uanse'lig* insignificant (but *u'adelig* not of nobility), *utvi'vlsom* indubitable. Note further the adjectives *uvi'dende* ignorant, *umæ'lende* speechless, *ue'nig* of a different opinion, *ukri'stelig* un-Christian, the conjunction *ua'gtet* although, and the verbs *uma'ge* (or *u'mage*) and *ulei'lige* to trouble.

74. The prefixes *mis-*, *sam-*, *und-*, *van-*, *veder-* as a rule have the accent; Ex.: *Mi'sdæder* evildoer, *Sa'marbejde* co-operation, *u'ndsige* to defy, *Va'n-art* wickedness, *Ve'derlag* compensation, but adjectives derived in -*elig* and -*som* takes the accent on the second part of the composition: *mistæ'nksom* suspicious (but *Mi'stanke* suspicion), *undgaa'elig* avoidable, *vedersty'ggelig* abominable; and so do the following words: *Misu'ndelse* envy, *Undta'gelse* exception, *Undvi'gelse* or *U'ndvigelse* escape, *undta'gen* except (but with inverted position of the words: *e'n alene u'ndtagen* one only excepted), *undvæ'rlig* dispensable, *samdræ'gtig* unanimous, *vana'rtig* wicked, *vanku'ndig* ignorant.

SENTENCE ACCENT.

75. Different from the syllabic accent is the sentence or rhetoric accent, whereby a different stress is given to the different words of the sentence according to their logical importance.

Pronouns, prepositions, conjunctions and other particles as well as auxiliary verbs are as a rule unaccented. When a word is used in the sentence without stress it is subject to different changes, such as abbreviation of long sounds, loss of glottal stop (see § 76) and even loss of a part of their substance (see §§ 65 and 16).

Sometimes the whole meaning of a sentence is changed by a change of accent: *Min Ven gi'k igen* my friend left again, *min Ven gik ige'n* my friend reappeared (as a ghost, haunted the house).

GLOTTAL STOP.

76. The accent stress (including in some cases the secondary accent) takes in Danish in a great many (originally) monosyllabic words the peculiar form of a **glottal stop** or **catch** (Sweet), by the Danish grammarians called *Stødtone* or *Tonehold*. This glottal stop is produced by a temporary closure of the glottis and a corresponding interruption of the voice, the result being a sound very similar to the one produced by cough or hiccough. Those Danish dialects, therefore, which are especially given to the use of the glottal stop are said to "hiccough the words forth". As the glottal stop consists in an interruption of the voice, it results that it can only occur in sounds that are produced or accompanied by an emission of voice (vowels and voiced consonants).

The accent stress of originally polysyllabic words is characterized by the absence of the glottal stop.

[The glottal stop is here indicated by (*).]

77. The glottal stop chiefly occurs in the following cases (although there is some difference between the various dialects and also individually as to its use):

1) a great many monosyllables: *Ma*nd* man, *Hu*s* house, *faa** few (always in monosyllables consisting of long vowel sound followed by consonant (excepting *Fa'r*, *Mo'r*, *Bro'r*, *Pe'r*, *Pov'l* which are originally dissyllabic) or short vowel

sound followed by two voiced consonants; as a rule in those ending in a long vowel or diphthong; those consisting of short vowels followed by *h, m, n, ny* with following voiceless consonant take the glottal stop in the dialect of Sealand, but not in that of Jutland, while *r* in this position is incompatible with glottal stop; sometimes it occurs in words having a short vowel before one single voiced consonant).

2) many dissyllables in *-el, -en* and *-er*; Ex.: *Æ*sel* donkey, *Vin*ter* winter, *A*sen* donkey.

3) the radical syllable of many compound verbs, adjectives, adverbs and nouns derived from verbs, where the glottal stop is lacking in the non-compound words: Ex.: *(h)jemsø*ge* to visit, *Me'dskyl*dig* accomplice, *Ankla*ger* accuser.

4) in some foreign words: *Kano*n, Stude*nt, Ame*rika*.

78. The glottal stop serves to distinguish pairs of words which otherwise would have the same sound:

1) the definite form of monosyllables from that of dissyllables ending in *-e*, the former with, the latter without glottal stop.

with glottal stop	without glottal stop
Aan*den the spirit (*Aand*)	*Aand'en* the breath (*Aande*)
Skø*det the lap (*Skød*)	*Skø'det* the deed (of conveyance, *Skøde*)
Bun*den the bottom (*Bund*)	*Bond'en* the peasant (*Bonde*)

2) the plural form of monosyllables, ending in *-er* (with stop) and of dissyllables, ending in *-r* (without stop).

with stop	without stop
Æn*der ducks (*And*)	*End'er* ends (*Ende*)
Stæn*ger sticks (*Stang*)	*Stæng'er* hay-lofts (*Stænge*)

3) the definite form of monosyllabic substantives (with stop) and corresponding adjectives or participles (without stop).

    with stop   without stop

Sej*let the sail   *sejl'et* sailed
Stø*vet the dust   *støv'et* dusty

4) past participle plural of some weak verbs (with stop) and the corresponding imperfect tense (without stop): Ex.:

(*de bleve*) *pi*nte* they were tortured; (*de*) *pi'nte* they tortured;

5) some proper nouns (with stop) and corresponding appellatives (without stop).

    with stop   without stop

En*gel   *Eng'el* angel
Jæ*ger   *Jæ'ger* hunter
Kri(e)*ger   *Kri'ger* warrior
Møl*ler   *Møll'er* miller

6) present tense of some verbs (with stop) and the corresponding nouns (without stop):

    with stop   without stop

(*han*) *mal*er* he paints   *Mal'er* painter
"   *lø*ber* he runs   *Løb'er* runner

7) the definite form of some monosyllabic substantives (with stop) and verbal nouns ending in *-en* (without stop);

Tviv*len the doubt   *Tviv'len* doubting
Sme*den the smith   *Sme'den* forging.

QUANTITY OF DANISH SOUNDS.

79. Vowels and open consonants can be long or short; shut consonants (stops) are in the Danish language always short.

Long sounds can only occur in accentuated syllables. A consonant written double between two vowels indicates that the preceding vowel is short, but final consonants are n o t written double to indicate shortness of preceding vowel except in a few cases where it may be done, when it is thought desirable to distinguish between two words that otherwise would look alike; Ex.: *Brud(d)* rupture, *Brud* bride, *Dug(g)* dew, *Dug* table cloth.

NOTE. In the following words consonants are written double after a long vowel to indicate the hard (non-spirantic) sound: *Drægge* grapnels, *dægge* to coddle, *Hæggen* the bird cherry, *Læggen* the calf, *Lægget* the fold, tuck, *Plaggen* the colt, *Skægget* the beard, *Væggen* the wall, *Æggen* the edge, *Ægget* the egg, *Næbbet* the beak *Bredde* breadth, *Vidde* width. The vowel is also long before double consonant in the following words: *otte* eight, *sjette* sixth, *Sotten* the sickness, *Ætten* the family, and in words derived by the termination *-mæssig: forholdsmæssig* proportionate, etc.

80. The quantity of consonants is not indicated in spelling. Long is the first of two soft consonants (*l, m, n, r, d, g*) in intermediate position between two vowels, the preceding vowel then being short, accentuated and pronounced without glottal stop: *hamre* to hammer, *hornet* horned, *Almagt* omnipotence, *Stenbord* stone table. (But short consonant in *ramse* to say by rote, *Skjorte* shirt, *Hor*net* the horn).

NORWEGIAN SOUNDS.

81. Table of the Norwegian vowels classified according to their place of articulation.

		BACK.		MIXED		FRONT.	
		Not rounded.	Rounded.	Not rounded.	Rounded.	Not rounded.	Rounded.
HIGH	Narrow		o		u	i	y
	Wide						
MID	Narrow		å·			e	ø
	Wide		å			ä	ö
LOW	Narrow					æ	œ
	Wide	a					

For the explanation of the technical terms: Back, Mixed, Front, High, Mid, Low, see § 10.

NOTE. *a* is a little advanced, but not so much so as in Danish. Vulgarly and dialectically the long *a* may be pronounced further back and with a slight rounding, approaching the English *aw* in *law*.

o is midway between *high* and *mid* and *å* midway between *mid* and *low*, but both are pronounced with the rounding corresponding to the higher stage.

ACOUSTIC VALUE OF THE NORWEGIAN VOWELS.

82. *a* has the sound of English *a* in father, short or long. Ex. short: *Hat* hat, *Man(d)* man; long: *Dag* day, *Sal* hall.

83. æ has the sound of English *a* in *care*; it occurs long or short before *r*; Ex. long: *bære* to bear, *lære* to teach, *nær* near; short: *Færd* conduct, voyage, *Smerte* pain, *Verk* work.

NOTE. The orthographic sign of this sound may be, as seen from the above examples, *æ* or *e;* the former is used when the same word in another form or another kindred word has *a* or *aa* where the word in question has æ; Ex.: *Færd* derived from *fare* to travel, *bære* to carry, impf. *bar; færre* fewer, comp. of *faa; Kærring* old (or married) woman derived from *Kar(l)* man. Where this rule does not apply, i. e. where there is no such *a* or *aa* to judge by, then the long *a*-sound as a rule is written *æ*, the short *e*. But there are some exceptions. Ex. long sound written *e: der* there, *er* is, *Erende* message, *fjerde* fourth, *her* here, *igjer(d)e* (or *igjære*) going on, *Jern* iron, *Jertegn* sign, miracle. Short sound written *æ: fordærve* to spoil, *forfærde* to frighten; *særdeles* especially, *værd* (colloquially pronounced *vært*) worth, *værre* worse.

Obs. *Veir* weather, pron. *vær*

84. ä long or short, like English *e* in "men"; Ex. short: *ret* right, *slet* even, bad, *træt* tired; long: *Glæde* joy, *Fædre* fathers, *Stæder* cities.

Orthographic signs of the sound ä are *æ* and *e;* their use corresponds to the rule given in § 83 note. Exceptions: a) long ä written *e: Eventyr* fairy tale, *ihje'l* to death, *Kjede* chain, *vever* agile; b) short ä written *æ: Dræg* grapnel, *Væg* wall, *Græs* grass, *hæslig* ugly, *lemlæste* to maim, *Væske* satchel, *Væ(d)ske* fluid, *ræd* afraid, *træt* tired, *Kjæft* (vulgar) mouth, *Tæft* scent, *Kræft* cancer, *Blæk* ink, *lække* to leak, *Læk* leak, *Spræk* crack, *sprække* to crack, *Fælle* fellow, *Træl* thrall, *Væld* spring, *Vælde* power, *(H)vælv* vault, *Kjælke* sled, *Frænde* relative, *ænse* to mind, *faafængt* useless, *forfængelig* vain, *Hævd* prescriptive right.

NOTE. In the dialect of Christiania and the southern part of Norway the long sound of ä has been replaced by the long *e*, and the short sound of ä is only half wide.

85. *e* like French *é* in "*été*", English *a* in "name" as usually pronounced in America, i. e. without the diphthongic element. Short *e* only occurs in words formed by inflection or derivation from words with long *e;* Ex.: *bre(d)t* neuter form of *bre(d)* broad, *Bredde* breadth, derived from the same word; Ex. long: *Te* tea, *Ve(d)* wood, *hed* (pron. het) hot.

Orthographic sign of this sound is *e*.

NOTE. In the dialect of Christiania and the southern part of Norway the long sound of *e* has been substituted for that of ä, see § 84 note. On the other hand the short sound of *e* is in the speech of many, even educated, people in the course of being replaced by a half wide short ä. As yet, however, the pronounciation of *brät* instead of *bre(d)t* may be considered as bordering on the vulgar.

86. *i* short or long; it has the narrow sound of English *ee* in "see"; Ex. long: *Vin* wine, *ti* ten, *i* in; short: *Vin(d)* wind, *li(d)t* (neut.) little. Orthographic sign *i*, except in the word *de* (*De*) they, the, you.

NOTE. For the pronunciation of *mig, dig, sig* see § 94. Before vowels *i* as a rule is pronounced so very short as to make it almost or wholly consonantic in character: *Kastanie* (pron. *Kastarje*) chestnut, *Familie* (j) family, *Kristiania* (j, or as a very short i); as a short i also in *Kariol* carriole, *Million;* *tredie* the third is pronounced *tredde* or *tredje*.

87. ə has the sound of German unaccented *e* in "Gabe," approaching French *e* in "que"; but often its articulation is more advanced and then it sounds almost like a short *e*. This is especially often the case in unaccented prefixes. ə only occurs in unaccented syllables; orthographic sign e; Ex.: *Gave* gift, *være* to be, *befale* (ə-a-ə) to order.

NOTE. the orthographic sign for ə is *i* or *e* in *tusin(d)* or *tusen(d)* thousand.

88. å has a sound approaching English *a* in *call* (but it is pronounced with a somewhat higher articulation; raised low or lowered mid; the rounding is the same as corresponds to the mid sound (*o*) in the European languages generally. It may be long or short, the short sound being somewhat wider than the long one.

NOTE 1. Orthographic sign of the long sound is as a rule *aa* (å); Ex : *Aal* eel, *graa* grey, *Vaar* spring.

Exceptions: before *g* and *v* the sound of å is usually written *o*: *over* over, *doven* lazy, *love* to promise, *Skov* forest, *og* and, *Sprog* language; but if *g* represents the sound of *k* (see § 122), then the sound of å is written *aa* (å): *Maage* mew, pron. *måke* (or *måge*), *Taage* (*k*) fog, *vaage*(*k*) to wake, *vaagen* awake; also in *Vaag* (*g*) bay, *Aag* (*g*) yoke. Observe also *Fole* (å) colt, *Torsdag* (å) Thursday, *vor* (å) our, *fore* a prefix (*forebygge* to prevent, *Foremers* foretop).

NOTE 2. The orthographic sign of the short sound as a rule is *o*; Ex.: *Lod* half an ounze, *holde* to hold, *Konge* king. Exceptions: *aa* is as a rule written before *nd*, representing the sound *nn*: *Baan*(d) ribbon, *Haan*(d) hand; in the words *Aadsel* carcass, *fraadse* gourmandize, and others; furthermore in forms or words derived from corresponding words with a long *aa*; Ex.: *graat* neut. of *graa* grey, *haar*(d)*t* neut. of *haar*(d) hard, etc.

89. *o* has no exact equivalent outside of the Scandinavian languages, although it comes very near to the sound of English *oo* in "poor." Its place of articulation is midway between "high" and "mid," and the rounding corresponds to high (*oo*). It may be short or long. Orthographic sign for the long sound is *o*, for the short *o* or *u*; Ex. long: (*jeg*) *lo* (I) laughed, *Horn* horn, *Hob* multitude; Ex. short: *Bonde* peasant, *op* up (in Christiania pronounced åp), *Buk* (*o*) he-goat, *tung* (*o*) heavy. *u* serves to represent this sound before *ng*, *nk* and as a rule before *m* ending a syllable or followed by another consonant, *f*, *k* and *gt*. Furthermore in the following words: *Kunst* art, *Spuns* bung. *Kul*, coal, is sometimes pronounced *kol*.

90. Also the Scandinavian *u* is a peculiar sound without any exact equivalent in English. It comes nearest to the English *u* in "full" or "put." In pronouncing the Norwegian *u* the back of the tongue is raised towards the hard palate and the point remains behind the lower incisors, while the lips are considerably protruding. Ex. long: *Gud* God, *Ur* watch, *hul* (adj.) hollow, *Brud* bride; short: *Brud* breach, *Gut* boy, *Hul* hole (also pronounced *Hol*).

NOTE. For *u* being the orthographic sign of *o* see § 89.

91. *y* has the tongue position of *i*, the lip rounding of *u*. It sounds like German ü, French *u* in "lune," only still thinner, nearer to *i*. It may be short or long. Phonetic sign *y*. Ex. long: *By* town, *syv* seven, *yde* yield; short: *yppe* to raise, *yste* to make cheese, *bygge* to build.

NOTE. For *y* being sometimes pronounced as ö see § 92 note.

92. ø ö.

ø is a rounded *e* and has a sound like French *eu* in "peu"; it only occurs long, but is never found before radical *r*; Ex.: *Ø* island, *dø* die, (*Hunden*) *gjør* (the dog) barks. ö is a rounded œ and has a sound like French *eu* in "peuple," German *ö* in "Götter." It occurs both short and long, long only before radical *r*. In this latter position, however, the dialect of Christiania has a still lower (more open) sound œ. Ex. ö: *sö(d)t* sweet (neut.), *grön* green; *ö* or œ: *Börn* or *Bœrn* children, *gjör* or *gjœr* does, *hörlig* or *hœrlig* audible.

NOTE. The orthographic sign of all three sounds, ø, ö and œ is in print as a rule ø, in writing ö.

In a few words the sign *y* represents the sound of ö: *sytten* (ö) 17, *sytti* (ö) 70, *fyrti* (ö, œ) 40. Also in some other words *y* may be pronounced as ö: *Lykke* luck, *Stykke* piece, *Bryst* breast, *flytte* to move. But the pronunciation as *y* is regularly heard among educated people.

NORWEGIAN DIPHTHONGS.

93. The diphthongic sounds occurring in the Norwegian language are: *ai, æi, oi, öi, œu*. *ai* has a sound like English *i* in "mile." Ex.: *Hai* shark, *Kai* quay, *vaie* wave, float. In the word *Mai* May, *a* as a rule is pronounced long.

94. *æi* has the orthographic sign *ei*, which sign always represents the sound here indicated (not as in Danish: *ai*); Ex.: *lei* tedious, disagreeable; *Vei* road.

In some words *eg, ek, ig* serve as signs for this diphthongic sound: *jeg* I (pron. jæi), *mig* me, *dig* you, *sig* himself etc. (pron. *mæi* etc.). *seksten* 16 (pron. *sæisten*).

egl, egn are in the greater part of Norway pronounced *æil, æin*; but in the northern part *egn* is pronounced *engn*; Ex.: *Negl* (*æi*) nail, *Tegl* (*æi*) tile, *Regn* (*æin* or *engn*) rain. In mathematics distinction is made between *Kegle* cone and *Kile* wedge, lat. cuneus. But in everyday speech both words are pronounced alike; *slaa kjiler* (i. e *Kegler*) play at ninepins, *slaa ind en kjile* (i. e. *Kile*) drive in a wedge.

95. *oi* only occurs in some foreign words; it has the same sound as English *oy* in "boy," but has a tendency to become assimilated with *öi*: *holloi* halloo, *Konvoi* convoy.

96. In *öi* the first element of the diphthong is the wide *ö*, the second a wide *y*; Ex.: *höi* high, *Töi* cloth, *föite* to gad. *ög* in *Lögn* lie, *Dögn* day and night, as a rule represents the same sound, but in the northern part of the country those words are pronounced *löngn, döngn*. *Nögel* key is by some people pronounced *nøiel*, commonly *nökkel*.

The word *Bygd* country township is sometimes pronounced *böid*, but usually as it is spelt. The former pronunciation is still considered somewhat vulgar, although I b s e n uses it in "B r a n d" in the following rhyme:

Tusen fulgte mig af Bygden (öi),
ikke én vandt op til Höiden.

The sound of *öi* is in some foreign words represented by e u: *Farmaceut* (pron. *söit*) pharmacist, *Lieutenant* (pron. and now regularly spelt *löitnant*), *neutral* (*öi*) neuter, *Eugen* (pron. *öisjén*).

97. *œu* has a sound that comes very near the Cockney pronunciation of *ou* in "house." Orthographical sign *au*. Ex.: *taus* silent, *August*, *Taug* rope.

This diphthong is written *eu* in *Europa*. (But in Greek names *Zeus* etc. *eu* is pronounced *ev*).

NORWEGIAN CONSONANTS.

98. *p* as in English; Ex.: *Pave* pope, *Penge* money, *Pil* arrow, *op* up.

NOTE 1. Vulgar is a tendency to pronounce *p* before *t* as *f*; Ex.: *kaftein* for *Kaptein* Captain, *skaft* for *skapt* (written *skabt*) shaped.

NOTE 2. The sound of *p* is written *b* in the following cases:

1) after short vowel before, mostly inflective, *t* and *s*: *skabt* (*p*) shaped, *raabt* (pron. *ropt*) called, *Krebs* (*p*) crawfish, *Skibshund* (*p*) ship's dog, *Labskaus* (*p*) lobscouse: *Læbe* lip is often pronounced *leppe*, with short vowel.

2) after a long vowel when *p* either ends a word or is followed by *ə* (see § 6 in fine); Ex.: *Gab* (*p*) yawn, *gabe* (*pə*) to yawn, *Skrab* (*p*) trash, *skrabe* (*p*) to scrape, *Skab* (*p*) wardrobe, *Tab* (*p*) loss, *tabe* (*p*) to lose, *Kaabe* (*p*) cloak, *taabelig* (*b* or *p*) foolish, *krybe* (*p*) to creep. Among the younger generation of authors it is getting always more common to spell these words in accordance with the Norwegian pronunciation. It is only in a small part of the coast districts in the southernmost part of Norway that *b* in these words is pronounced as written, similarly to the pronunciation in Danish (see § 4).

99. *b* sounds like English b; this sound occurs in the beginning, middle (chiefly in foreign words) and end of words; Ex.: *By* town, *Bly* lead, *Hybel* garret, *Lab* (pr. labb) paw.

NOTE. Sometimes *b* interchanges with *p* after a long vowel (see § 98 Note 2), *b* being reserved for a more elevated style or a figurative meaning; Ex.:

p.	b.
döbe, p, to baptize.	*Daab, b*, baptism; *Johannes den Döber* John the Baptist.
gribe, p, to catch.	figuratively: *en gribende Scene* an impressive scene.
raabe (pr. rope) to call aloud, cry.	*raabe* in some sentences figuratively: *hans Forbrydelse raaber om Hævn* his crime cries for vengeance.
Raab (*raap, rop*) cry, call.	*Raab, b: Raabet paa Reformer* the clamor for reforms. *Raaber* a speaking trumpet.
skröbelig, p, fragile, frail.	figuratively: *Kjödet er skröbeligt, b*, the flesh is weak.
tabe, p, to lose.	*fortabes, b* (theol.) to be damned; *et Fortabelsens Barn* a child of perdition.
sleben, p, ground, cut (*slepet Glas*, cut glass).	*et slebent, b, Væsen* a polished address.
skabe, p, sig to act in an affected manner.	*skabe, b*, to create; *Skabelse* creation.
Svöbe (pr. *Svepe*) driving whip.	*Svöbe, öb*, scourge.
—*skab, p*, in *Ondskab, p*, evilness, *Troldskab, p*, witchcraft; *Ægteskab, p*, marriage.	—*skab, b*, in *Kundskab* (also *p*) knowledge, *Videnskab, b*, science.

100. *m* bilabial nasal, like the English m; Ex.: *maa* must, *om* about, *komme* to come. Before *f m* assumes a labiodental character, more rarely before *v*; Ex.: *Jomfru* young woman, stewardess.

101. *f* is a labiodental open sound like English f; Ex.: *faa* get, *puffe* to push.

NOTE 1. In the word *af* of *f* is a sign for the sound of *v*, see § 102, Note 1.

NOTE 2. In inflective forms of words, the stems of which end in "v" the sound of *f* is sometimes written "v": *havt* (partcp.) pron. *haft* had (colloquially pron. hat); see § 102 Note 2.

102. v is a labiodental open voiced sound, not quite so sharply articulated as English *v*. Occurs both in the beginning, middle and at the end of words; Ex.: *vi* we, *love* to promise, *Skov* forest.

NOTE 1. In the word *af* of this sound has the orthographic sign *f*.

NOTE 2. v is the orthographic sign of the sound *f* 1) before *s* and *t* in inflective forms of words, the stems of which end in *v*, when the vowel preceding *v* is short; if the preceding vowel is long, then *v* retains its sound; in some words both pronunciations (long vowel & *v* and short vowel &*f*) are admissible; Ex.: *sætte tillivs* (*f*) to dispatch (food); *Livsens* (*f*) of life, *grovt* (*v* or *f*) rough (neuter form), *paaskrevs* (*v* or *f*) astride, *tilhavs* (*v* or *f*) at sea. Also *revse* (*f*) to castigate. Colloquially the imperfect *lovede* promised is pronounced *lofte*. 2) In the words: *Viol* (flower) *v*iolet, *V*iolin, *V*ioloncel.

NOTE 3. v is written but not pronounced after *l* in *hal*(v) half, *sel*(v) self, *Söl*(v) silver, *tol*(v) twelve, *tol*(v)*te* twelfth, *Tyl*(v)*t* dozen; furthermore in *Pro*(v)*st* dean, *Tvi*(v)*l* doubt (now regularly written Tvil), *ha*(v)*t* had, *bra*(v) or *brav*, plural pronounced *brave* or *bra*.

For *bli*(ve)*r gi*(ve)*r* see § 140 c.

103. *t* is a voiceless dental stop, slightly aspirated, especially in the beginning of words, but much less so than in Danish. The aspiration is omitted after *s*, *t* in this position thus representing a sound between *t* and *d*; Ex.: *Tal* number, *Hat* hat, *Potet* potato, *stor* big.

th does not represent any other sound than *t*; it is used in some words of Greek origin and as a rule in the conjunction *thi* for, to distinguish it from the numeral *ti* ten, both words being pronounced alike. Sometimes also in *Thing* Session of court, *Storthing* name of Norwegian parliament, to distinguish these words from *Ting* thing; furthermore in *Throndhjem*, *Thorsdag* Thursday; but these words are now generally spelt without *h*.

Note 1. *t* is written but not pronounced 1) in *de(t)* that, the (pron. art.) and in the enclitic definite article neuter; Ex.: *Huse(t)* the house. In elevated speech, however, the *t* in this latter case usually retains its sound.

2) in the words *Gjes(t)giver* country innkeeper, *Vær(t)shus* inn.

3) in the infinitive particle *at* to, colloquially pronounced å, thus distinguished from the conjunction *at* that, pronounced as written. In stead of *Disputats* disputation, *Notits* notice, etc., it is now the rule to write *Disputas*, *Notis*, etc.

Note 2. For *tj* in some words representing the sound of *kj* see § 119 Note.

104. The sound of *t* is represented by the sign *d* in many words finally and before ə after a long vowel; Ex.: *blød (t)* soft, *bide (t)* to bite, *Baad (t)* boat, *kaad (t)* jolly, *vaad (t)* wet, *Flaade (t)* raft, *Maade (t)* manner, (but *Saate* hay-cock also spelt with *t*, because it is a distinctly Norwegian word), *Fad (t)* dish, *flad (t)* flat, *Gade (t)* street, *lad (t)* lazy, *Mad (t)* food, *fed (t)* fat, *Gjed (t)* goat, *hed (t)* hot, *hede (t)* to be called, *lede (t)* to search, *Hvede (t)* wheat, *Sæde (t)* seat (but *gjæte* to guard (grazing animals) spelt with *t* cfr. *Saate*), *did (t)* thither, *hvid (t)* white, *hid (t)* hither, *liden (t)* little, *Fod (t)* foot, *mod (t)* against, *Bod (t)* amende, *Rod (t)* root, *rode (t)* to rummage, *Sod (t)* soot, *Grud (t)* grounds, *lude (t)* to stoop, *Knude (t)* knot, *Lud (t)* lye, *Pude (t)* pillow, *Stud (t)* oxe, *tude (t)* to toot, *Tud (t)* spout, *ud (t)* cut, *ude (t)* out, *bryde (t)* break, *Gryde (t)* pot, *Lyde (t)* blemish, *skryde (t)* to boast, *skyde (t)* to shoot, *snyde (t)* to blow (the nose), *bøde (t)* to pay a fine, *Bøder (t)* fines, *Fløde (t)* cream, *Grød (t)* porridge, *møde (t)* meeting, *Stød (t)* push, *støde (t)* to push, *Skjøde (t)* deed of conveyance.

Double consonant after short vowel: *Nod* pron. *Nött* nut, *Fodder* feet, pron. *Fötter*, *sidde* to sit, pron. *sitte*.

NOTE. For some of these words in specific meanings being pronounced with *d*, see § 106.

105. *d* like English *d;* Ex.: *da* then, *blodi(g)* bloody, *ræd* (*dd*) afraid.

NOTE. Where the Danish and the common Norwegian orthography have *d* in the end or middle of words after a long vowel, the common Norwegian pronunciation as a rule either has *t* or drops the *d*. In the former case *d* corresponds to ON. *t* (see §§ 4 & 6), in the latter to ON. ð.

106. Some words written with *d* are pronounced with *d* or *t* according to the meaning. The voiced explosive as a rule occurs in learned words and those chiefly occurring in higher style.

t.

flyde, t, to float, to flow.
græde, t (*gråte*) to cry, to weep.
Kjöd, tt, meat.
lide, t, to trust.

Maade, t, manner.

nyde, t, to take (food), *nyde, t, godt af noget* to draw profit of something.
raadden, tt, rotten, putrid.
Mod, t, courage.
Flade, d or *t,* plane.
Skjöd, t, lap (*Frakkesjöd* coatlap), *Skjödskind* (shoemaker's) apron.
vide, t, to know.

d.

flydende d, liquid.
begræde, d, to cry over.
Kjöd, d, flesh.
Tillid, d, trust, *paalidelig, d,* trustworthy.
NOTE. Always *lide, d,* to suffer.
Maade, d, mode (gram.); *Tak i lige Maade* thanks, the same to you.
nyde, d, to enjoy, *nydelig* enjoyable, pretty.

raadden (morally) foul.
modig, courageous.
always *overfladisk* superficial.
i Familiens Skjöd in the bossom of the family.

Videnskab science, *Viden* knowledge.

t.

ydre, tt, outer; *Yderfrak, tt*, overcoat; *yderst, tt*, outermost.
bide t, to bite.
blöd, t, soft.
Flaade t, raft.
forbryde, t, sig to offend, trespass.

lade, t, let; *lade som om* to make it appear that. (See also § 140).
overlade, t, to leave; *tillade, t*, to allow.

d.

yderst utmost, *den yderste Dag* the day of judgment.
bidende pungent (answer, speech).
blödagtig effeminate.
Flaade fleet.
Forbryder criminal, *Forbrydelse* crime.

lades det maa man lade ham, it must be admitted that he.
tilsyneladende apparently, *Tilladelse* permission.

107. *d* is often written at the end or in the middle of words after a long vowel without being pronounced (see § 105 Note). In rhetoric language the *d* may be retained in pronunciation, and in some words there are duplicate forms with or without *d* according to the meaning.

Without d.

Bla(d) leaf, sheet, newspaper

bli(d) gentle, bland.
Blo(d) blood, *at spytte Blo(d)* to spit blood, *blo(d)rö(d)* red as blood.

bre(d) broad: *der skal en bre(d) Ryg til at bære gode Dage* it takes a broad back to carry god fortune.
Brö(d) bread.

With d.

Nordiske Blade (name of newspaper), *ta(ge) Bladet fra Munden* to speak one's mind.
dit blide Aasyn your sweet face.
Kjöd og Blod flesh and blood, *Blodets Baand* the ties of blood; in many compounds: *Blodbad* carnage, *Blodhevn* revenge for murder, *Blodskam* incest.
de brede Bygder the broad parishes.

vort daglige Bröd our daily bread; *den enes Död, den andens Bröd* one man's death, the other man's breath (literally: bread).

Without d.	With d.
dö(d) dead; (colloquially may be used the genuine Norwegian form *dau* in the meaning of sluggish).	*Död* death; *död og magteslös* nulland void; *d* is always pronounced when the adjective is used as a noun: *en död* a dead man, *staa op fra de döde* to rise from the dead.
Flo(d) high tide.	*Flod* river.
gla(d) joyous.	*et glad Budskab* glad tidings, *en glad Aften* a merry night.
go(d) good.	*den gode* the good man, *et Gode* a blessing.
Raa(d) means, expedient: *der er ingen Raa(d) med ham* there is no outcome with him, *det er ikke Raa(d)* it is not possible, *jeg har ikke Raa(d)* I cannot afford, *raa d̦lös* without an expedient.	*Raad* advice, *en Statsraad* (king's) minister, *Kongens Raad* the king's council, *raadföre sig med en* to seek somebody's advice.
rö(d) red, *en rö(d) Næse* a red nose.	*han er röd* he is red (i. e. radical in politics), *de röde Hunde* the red dogs (i. e. roseola).
stri(d), adj. headstrong.	*Strid*, subst. strife.
Ti(d) time, in *go(d) Ti(d)* plenty of time, *alti(d)* always.	*Tid* time, usual form.
vi(d) wide, *en vi(d) Frakke* a wide coat.	*en vid Horisont* a wide horizon (i. e. scope of ideas), *uden videre* without further ado.

109. *d* is always pronounced in *Bad* bath, *Bod* booth, *Bryderi* trouble, *Daad* deed, *Ed* oath, *Fraade* foam, *Fred* peace, *Gröde* crop, *Gud* God, *Had* hate, *Hæder* honor' *led* loathsome, *Lyd* sound, *Naade* grace, *Odel* allodial ownership; as a rule in *Bud* message, always when this word indicates messenger.

d also as a rule is pronounced in derivatives; Ex.: *fredelig* peaceful, *Glæde* joy, *raadelig* advisable.

109. *nd* and *ld* are as a rule pronounced *nn* and *ll: Mand* (*nn*) man, *Mund* (*nn*) mouth, *kold* (*ll*) cold, *Kulde* (*lle*) subst. cold, *holde* (*lle*) to hold, *volde* (*lle*) to cause.

d is pronounced as *d* after *l* before *r: Alder* age, *Bulder* noice, *Hulder* wood nymph, *Skulder* shoulder; and in the following words: *Gilde* company, *hilde* to snare, *Kilde* fountain, *Olding* old man, *Ælde* age, *Vælde* power; furthermore in derivative words when the ending commences in a vowel: *gylden* golden, *heldig* fortunate (but *Hel*(*d*) fortune).

d is pronounced after *n* before *r* and *l: andre* others, *handle* to deal, *Handel* (pr. *handl*) a deal; *d* is also pronounced in derivatives: *sandelig* verily, *sandig* sandy; also as a rule in *Kvinde* woman, *Minde* reminiscence; *jeg har i Sinde* I have in mind (but *jeg gjorde det i Sinne* I did it in anger), *Kunde* customer.

110. *d* is mute 1) before *s* a) after a short vowel, in which case *ds* is pronounced *ss*: *be*(*d*)*st* best, *Bi*(*d*)*sel* bridle, *bi*(*d*)*sk* snappish, *Pla*(*d*)*s* place, *Kry*(*d*)*s* cross, hind quarter, *pu*(*d*)*sig* funny, and many others; b) in some words after a long vowel: *Lo*(*d*)*s* pilot, *lo*(*d*)*se* to pilot, *Seila*(*d*)*s* sailing, *Straba*(*d*)*s* (or *ts*) exertion; c) between *n* and *s: Bræn*(*d*)*sel* fuel, *min*(*d*)*ske* to decrease (the orthographic rule is to write *d* between *n* and *s* in the words derived from primitives with *d*: Ex.: *Han*(*d*)*ske* glove, from *Haand* hand; but *danse* to dance, *Grænse* limit, etc.); 2) before *t* when a *d* belonging to the stem comes before an inflective *t*: Ex.: *god—go*(*d*)*t* good, *blöd—blö*(*d*)*t* soft *lide—li*(*d*)*t* (part.) suffer; [before *t* of a derivative ending *d* is retained in writing when the ending consists of *t* alone; Ex.: *et Skri*(*d*)*t* a step, *et Ri*(*d*)*t* a ride; but changed into *t* when the ending consists of *t* with a following vowel: *god—gotte sig* to regal one's self.]

111. *d* is mute in some words after *r*; the preceding

vowel is usually long; Ex.: *Jor(d)* earth, *Fjor(d)* fjord, *Gjær(d)e* fence, *Or(d)* word, *Nor(d)mand* (short *o*) Norwegian.

In the following words *d* is pronounced after *r* (the preceding vowel in that case is short): *Bord* border, *Byrd* birth, *Færd* voyage (but *paafær(d)e* astir), *Hjord* herd, *hærde* to harden, *lærd* learned, *Mord* murder: *Verden* the world, *jorde* to inter, *Norden* the North, (but *nor(d)enfra* from the North, *nor(d)enfjelds* north of the mountains).

112. *s* is a voiceless open blade sound; the voiced (soft) *s* (*z*) of English and other languages does not exist in Norwegian; Ex.: *se* to see, *læse* to read, *Hus* house.

113. *sj* or *skj* have about the same sound as English *sh;* Ex.: *Sjö* sea, *sjelden* seldom, *Skjorte* shirt, *Skjört* skirt. Before *i* and *y* this sound is written *sk.* Ex.: *Ski* Norwegian snowshoe, *Sky* cloud; also before *e* in the following words: *Ske* spoon, (at) *ske* to happen, *maaske, kanske* (also pronounced *k*) perhaps, *Besked* information, *beskeden* modest, *skele* to squint, *Skelèt* skeleton, (at) *skeie* (ud) to lead a dissolute life; before *öi* in: *Sköite* smack, *Sköiter* skates (but *Sköi* fun, *Söier* mischiefmaker, with *k*).

The same sound may in foreign words be rendered by *sch, sh, g, ch, j, s,* according tho the spelling of the language from which the word is borrowed: *Chef, Geni, Bagage, jaloux, Journal, Kalesche. Brosche* brooch, *Punch, Schak* chess, *March, Revision, Mission, Addition, Direktion,* (but *Kvotient* pr. *kvotsient* in 3 syllables and *Konsortium* partnership, pr. *konsortsium* in 4 syllables).

114. *l* has about the same sound as in English; Ex.: *lide* to suffer, *Laar* thigh, *Pil* arrow, *spille* to play; for *ll* is in some words written *ld* (see § 109).

l is written but not pronounced before *j* in the words *Lja* or *Ljaa* scythe, *Ljore* opening in the roof for the smoke to pass out, *Ljom* echo, *Ljan* place near Christiania; furthermore in: *Karl* man, and its compounds (pronounced and often written *Kar*; *Stakkar* a wretch, Dan. *Stakkel*; but in

Huskarlene the housecarles pr. *l*); and in *skaI* shall, often pron. *ska*; and *til* to often pron. *te*.

NOTE. After point *r*, *l* in the eastern part of Norway assumes a supradental character, being formed against the gums, and *r* is reduced to a gliding sound; Ex : *Karl* (name), *farlig* dangerous, *Perle* pearl.

115. In eastern Norway the Old Norse combination *rð* has developed into a peculiar sound of inverted *r* or *l*, being pronounced by inverting the tongue and raising the point up towards the hard palate and then bringing it forward with a smack. The inverted or "cacuminal" sound produced in this manner makes upon the foreigner the impression of being an *r*, while to the Norwegians it appears to be an *l*; it is called the thick l; Ex.: *Svelvik* (O. N. *Sverðvik*), name of a place. This sound is considered vulgar, but it is often used colloquially in Eastern Norway, even instead of common *l*; Ex.: *Klasse* class, *Aal* eel, *Ola* (name).

116. *n* like English *n*: *nu* now, *Bön* prayer, *vænne* to accustom.

The sound of *nn* is written *nd* in a great many words (see § 109). Of words spelt with *nn* or *n* (if final) may be noted: *Bönne* bean, *Bön* prayer (plur. of both: *Bönner*, but *Bönder* peasants, with the same *n*-sound); *en Finne* a pimple, but *at finde* to find, *at kunne* to be able [but *jeg kunde* (*nn*) I could], *Skin* light, appearance (*at skinne* to shine), but *Skind* (*nn*) skin, *Skinne* rail, *Vantro* disbelief (but *Vandfarve* water color).

NOTE. When *n* is preceded by an *r*, then it in the eastern part of Norway assumes a supradental character, the *r* being reduced to a mere gliding sound. Other dental sounds are affected in the same way by a preceding *r*, and these combined sounds of *r* & following dental represent the same sounds that in the Sanskrit Grammar are called cerebral (murdhanja).

117. *ng* represent a single sound, the guttural nasal consonant, like English *ng* in s i n g e r; Ex.: *synge* to sing, *tung* heavy.

Before *k* the same sound is represented by *n* alone; Ex.: *Tanke* (*ngk*) thought, *Bœnk* bench.

The same is also sometimes the case before *g* in foreign words, *ng* thus representing the sound of *ngg*: *Kongo*, *Ungarn* Hungary; and in words of French origin also in other cases; Ex.: *balancere* (*ngs*) to balance. Sometimes also in compound words a *k* or *g* may affect a preceding dental *n* so as to make it guttural: *Huan(d)klæ(d,e* (*ngk*) towel; but as a rule both sounds remain the same as in the separate words; *Angiver* (*n-j*) informer, *angaa* (*n-g*) to concern. In some words of French origin *ng* is pronounced *ngsj* (*sj* representing the sound of Engl. *sh*, see § 113); Ex.: *rangere* pron. rangsjere, to rank, but *tangere* (*ngg*) to touch.

118. *r* in Norway as a rule is a trilled point consonant. Before a voice consonant or vowel it is voiced, before a voiceless consonant it is generally voiceless. It is formed by allowing the point of the tongue to vibrate against the gums while the breath of air passes trough. It is always distinctly pronounced, never modified like final *r* in English; Ex.: *Ry* fame, *Ror* rudder, *höre* to hear.

Note 1. In the south-western part of Norway is used an uvular *r*.

Note 2. The alveolar *r* exerts a peculiar influence on a following dental sound *t, d, l, n, s* (see §§ 114 note, 116 note). In polished language these supradental varieties of the front sounds as a rule are avoided after a short vowel as vulgar, except *rs*; Ex.: *Vers* verse (pron. almost versh), *Person* (pron. almost pershon).

119. *kj* is a medio-palatal fricative sound corresponding to German *ch* in i c h. The English language has no corresponding sound although the middle sound produced in English between *t* and *y* in such combinations as *not yet*, *don't you* has a certain resemblance to it. The sound is produced by raising the middle of the tongue towards the palate without touching it, while at the same time the point of the tongue is lowered behind the lower teeth and the side edges of the tongue touch the second molars. The orthographic sign is *kj* except before *i* and *y* when it is *k*; Ex.: *kjöre* to drive, *kjær* dear, *Kirke* church, *Kys* kiss. The sign of k represents this sound also before *e* in the words *Kegle* cone, *Kemi* chemistry, *Kerub*. (But *Keiser* emperor with *k*).

NOTE. The sound of *kj* is written *tj* in *Tjeld* oyster catcher (a bird), and *Tjern* a small lake, *Tjor* tether, *Tjære* tar.

120. *j* is the voiced sound corresponding to the voiceless *kj*, pronounced like English *y* in yawn.

This sound is represented 1) by *j*, usually; Ex.: *ja* yes, *jeg* (jei) I, *Jul* Christmas, *Mjö(d)* mead, *Linje* line, *tredje* (also pron. tredde) third, *Jöde* jew. 2) by *g* before *i* (except *Jib* jib, *jibbe* gybe) and sometimes before *y*; Ex.: *gift* married, *gik* went, *gylden* golden. (But *Jyde* Jutlander, *Jylland* Jutland. And in foreign words *g* may retain its proper sound before these vowels: *Gigant*, *Ægypten*, *Religion*; so also in *Gyda* woman's name) and sometimes in *give* (see § 140 c). 3) by *gj* sometimes before other vowels than the two above mentioned: *gjalde* to resound, *Gjed* (pron. je·t) goat, *jeg gjor(d)e* I did, *Gjæld* debt. 4) by *hj* in a few words; *Hjalte* hilt, *ihjel* to death, *Hjelm* helmet, *Hjem* Home, *Hjemmel* warrant, *Hjerne* brain, *Hjalmar*, *Hjerte* heart, *Hjord* herd, *Hjort* hart, *Hjul* wheel, *Hjælp* help, *Hjörne* corner. 5) by *lj* in *Ljaa*, *Ljore*, *Ljan* (see § 114).

(For *skj*, *sj* and *kj* see §§ 113 & 119).

121. *k* has the sound of English *k* but more aspirated; not so much so, however, as in Danish. The letter *k* represents this sound before consonants (except *j*, see § 119), back vowels (*a*, *o*, *u*) and unstressed front and mid vowels (*ə*, *i*) and at the end of words; Ex.: *kaste* to throw, *Klo* claw, *Knæ* knee (take care not to make the *k* mute as in English!), *Laks* salmon, *like* to like, *Viking*, *Raak* lane of water (cut in the ice), *Tak* (*kk*) thanks.

NOTE. When a word is spelt with *k* after a long vowel it is a sign that the word is originally Norwegian and does not occur in the Danish language. (See § 122).

122. The sound of *k* is in many words represented in writing by the letter *g*; 1) after a short vowel before *s* or *t*; 2) after a long vowel at the end of words or before *ə*; Ex.: 1) *Slags* (aks) kind (but *Slags* of a battle), *Krigsflaade* (ks) navy, *Rigs*(ks)-*advokat* attorney general, *bugsere* (ks) to tow, *Jagt* (kt) chase, *lagt* (kt) laid, *Digt* (kt) poem, *sligt* (kt) (neut.) such, *stygt* (kt) ugly, *stegt* (kt) ptc. fried, *Vægt* (kt) weight; 2) *Ager* (k) field, *bag* (k) behind, *Bager* (k) baker, *bruge* (k) to use, *Bøg* (k) beech, *Dug* (k) table cloth, *Hage* (k) chin, *Høg* (k) hawk, *Lage* (k) brine, *Lagen* (k) (bed)-sheet (but *Lager* (g) stock in store), *Leg* (k) play, *lege* (k) to play, *myg* (k) pliable [but *Myg* (gg) mosquito], *syg* (k) sick, *ryge* (k) to smoke (intr.), *røge* (k) to smoke (trans.), *Spiger* (k) nail, *Tag* (k) roof, grasp, *rig* (k) rich, *lig* (k) adj. like, *Forlig* (k or g) agreement, *forlige* (k or g) to reconcile [but *Forligelseskommission* (g) commissioners of arbitration], *Taage* (k) fog.

NOTE. Often in these words the pronunciations as *g* and *k* interchange with each other, the former being considered more polite and appropriate for elevated style.

In the following words there are double forms (with *k* and *g*) partly with a different meaning.

with *k*

Bog book pr. bo·k.
Flag sometimes pron. flak in *Isflag* flake of Ice, *Skjorteflag* (k or g) shirtlap.
klog (pr. klo·k) sagacious; *han er ikke rigtig klog* (k) he is not quite in his right senses, *jeg er lige* (k) *klog* (k) I am just as wise as I used to be.

with *g*.

Bog pr. Båg more polite.
Flag (a·g or agg) national ensign.

en klog (åg) *Kone* a wise woman (i.e. on supernatural things); *det er meget klogt gjort* that is a very clever move, *af Skade bliver man klog* damage makes wise.

Rige (k) empire, *et stort Rige* (k) a great empire.

Naturrigerne (g) the kingdoms of nature, *Guds Rige* (g) the kingdom of God, *det tyske Rige* the German empire, *Frankrige* (g) France (but *Sverige* pron. *Sverie* or *Sverje*, Sweden).

Sag (k) matter, *en farli(g) Sag* (k) a dangerous thing, *det er ingen Sag* (k) it is a very easy matter, *saysöge* (k, k) to sue.

Sagen the matter, *saglig* pertinent (strictly to the point), *Sagförer* lawyer.

NOTE: always *Sag* (g) saw.

Smag (k) taste, *en ubehageli(g) Smag* (k) *i Munden* (nn) a disagreeable taste in the mouth; *det har Mersmag* (k) it has a morish taste.

Smag (g) taste, *god Smag* good taste,
smagfuld(g, ll) tasteful, elegant,
Smagen er forskjellig taste differs.

vaage (k) to watch; *vaage* (k) *over en syg* to watch a sick person; *Vaage*(k)*kone* a sick-nurse.

vaager (g) *og beder* watch and pray.

Aag (sometimes pron. åk) yoke, oxbow.

gaa under Aaget (g) to walk under the yoke; *mit Aag* (g) *er gavnli(gt)*, my yoke is useful.

123. *k* is written but not pronouuced in the words: *Au*(*k*)*tion*, *Mul*(*k*)*t* fine, *mul*(*k*)*tere* to fine, *Engels*(*k*)*mand* Englishman; sometimes *k* is also dropped in pronouncing *Frans*(*k*)*mand* Frenchman, and always in *Frans*(*k*)*brö*(*d*) French rolls.

NOTE 1. For *k* being the orthographic sign of *kj* see § 119.

NOTE 2. There are still many people who instead of *ks* write *æ*; Ex.: *sexten* or *seksten* pron. seisten see § 94.

NOTE 3. The sound of *k* is still sometimes written *q* before *u*, pron. *kv*: *Quadrat* square, as a rule now written *Kvadrat*, *Aquavit* (pron. akkevit) Norwegian gin, now as a rule written *Akevit*.

124. *g* has the sound of English *g* in "give", "go"; Ex.: *gaa* to go, *gli(de)* to slide, *Gnier* miser, *grave* to dig, *jage* to hunt, *Norge* Norway, *Dag* day, *Sprog* (åg) language, *Tog* (åg) train, *Svælg* gullet, *Sorg* grief, *Helg* holidays, *Elg* elk, *Talg* tallow.

NOTE 1. In some of these words, after *l* and *r*, *g* is sometimes pronounced as *j*, but this pronunciation is considered vulgar.

NOTE 2. For *g* as the sign of k see § 122 note; for the pronunciation varying between *g* and k see § 122 note; for *g* and *gj* being signs of *j* see § 120, 2 and 3; *gid* would, o that, *gide* to prevail upon one's self to, are pronounced with *g* before *i*.

For *g* representing *i* as second part of diphthongs see §§ 94 and 96. For *g* representing the sound of *sj* in foreign words see § 113.

NOTE 3. *g* sometimes before *n* represents the sound of *ng*: *Agn* pron. angn, bait, *Magnus* pron. Mangnus or Magnus, *Vogn* pron. vongn. So also in the western and northern part of Norway in *Egn*, *Lögn* etc. (see § 94 and 96).

125. *g* is written but not pronounced:

1) in adjectives and adverbs ending in—ig (lig): *storagti(g)* haughty, *færdi(g)* ready, *aldri(g)* never: also when the plural ending *e* is added *g* remains mute; Ex.: *mærkeli(g)e Ting* strange things; and if the neutral ending *t* is added that also is mute: *Huse(t) er færdi(gt)* the house is ready.

2) after the diphthongs *ei* and *au*: *sei(g)* tough, *Dei(g)* dough, *Bau(g)* bow.

2) in the word *o(g)* and, and in some compounds of *Dag*: *godda(g)* good day (how do you do), *Manda(g)* Monday, *Tirsda(g)* Tuesday etc.; sometimes in *Ru(g)* (or *rugg*).

4) after a long vowel before *l*: *Fu(g)l* bird, *Ku(g)le* ball, *Pry(g)l* thrashing (but *g* always pronounced before *l* after a short vowel: Ex.: *Hagl* hail).

5) sometimes after *l* and *r* before an unstressed vowel:

imorges (rr) this morning, *imor(g)en* to-morrow. Sometimes the meaning changes according as *g* is pronounced or not:

g not pronounced:	*g* pronounced:
fölge (ll) to follow; *et Fölge* (ll) a company.	*en Fölge* (g) a consequence, *följende* following, *Följesætning* consequent (sentence), *följeværdig* worth following.
sælge (ll) to sell, *sol(g)te* sold.	*Sælger* (lg) a salesman.
spörge (rr) to ask, *Spör(g)smaal* question.	*spörgende* inquiring, *Spörgesætning* interrogative sentence.

126. *h* has before vowels the sound of English *h*; Ex.: *han* he, *Haab* hope, *holde* to hold, *hilse* to greet.

NOTE. A mute *h* is written before *j* and *v* in the following words: *Hjerne* brain, *Hjelm* helmet, *ihjel* to death, *Hjerte* heart, *Hjort* hart, *Hjord* herd, *Hjem* home, *Hjul* wheel, *Hjælp* help, *Hjörne* corner, *hva(d)* what, *hvem, hvo* who, *hvis* whose, if, *hvilken* which, *hvor* where (and compounds thereof *hvorfor* why etc.), *Hval* whale, *Hvalp* whelp, *hvas* sharp, *hvæsse* to whet, *Hvede* wheat, *Hveps* wasp, *hver* each, *Hverda(g)* week day, *hverken* neither, *Hverv* task, *hverve* to enlist, *hvid* white, *hvidte* to whiten, *Hvil* rest, *hvine* to shriek, *Hvirvel* whirlpool, *hviske* to whisper, *hvisle* to hiss, *Hvitting* whiting, *Hvælv* vault, *hvæse* to hiss.

NOTE. In the western and northern part of Norway the pronominal words spelt with *hv* are regularly pronounced with *k*: kem, ka etc., while some others are pronounced with *kv*: kvass, kvit, kvalp etc.

This pronunciation is not used by polite society, but the traveller may come across it.

127. *x* in some foreign words represents the sound of *ks* (many people still use this sign to express the same combination of sounds also in domestic words, see § 123 note 2); Ex.: *orthodox, Oxyd, extraordinær, Examen*. At the beginning of words of Greek origin it is usually pronounced *s*: *Xerxes* (pr. serses), *Xylograf*.

128. *z* is also used in some foreign words to represent the sound of *s*: *Zebra, Zelot.*

129. *e* is used in foreign words representing the sound of *s*; Ex.: *Ceder* cedar, *Centaur, Ceremoni, Cigar, musicere* to make music. In foreign words where it formerly was used to express the sound of *k* it is now the rule to write *k*. Greek proper nouns are now usually written and pronounced with *k*: *Kimon, Kyros.*

NORWEGIAN ACCENT.

130. In Norwegian speech a distinction must be made between the accent-stress and the musical accent.

131. The accent stress as a rule rests upon the first syllable, which at the same time generally is the radical syllable. A secondary stress is sometimes, especially in compound words, laid on o following syllable, i. e. in most cases on the first syllable of the second part of the compound; Ex.: *Bo'r(d)tœ'ppe* table cover, *La'mpeskjœ'rm* lampshade, *Gla'sme'ster* glazier. (' denotes primary accent, ' secondary accent).

132. The accent strees is on another syllable than the first.

1) in some foreign words; Ex.: *Genera'l, Cogna'c Apostro'f, Apothe'k.*

2) in words (of German origin) with the prefixes *be-, ge-, er-*, which never have the stress on the first syllable; Ex.: *begri'be* to understand, *Gevæ'r* shot-gun, *Gema'l* consort, *erfa're* to learn, *bekje'nde* to acknowledge, etc.

NOTE. In vulgar speech these words are accented on the first syllable; *bearbei'de* to adapt has usually the stress on the first syllable when meaning to belabor.

3) in some words with the prefix *for* representing the German *ver*; Ex.: *Forfa'tter* author, *forgaa' sig* to offend, *forfö're* to seduce, *Fornu'ft* reason; but: *fo'ranstalte* to cause to be done, *fo'rarbeide* to manufacture, *Fo'rbud* prohibition (but *forby'de* to prohibit), *Fo'rbund* alliance (but *forbi'nde sig* to agree), *Fo'rhold* relation (but *forho'lde sig* to behave), *Fo'rlag* publishing, *Fo'rlægger* publisher (but *forlæ'gge* to publish), *Fo'rmue* competency, *Fo'rsög* attemt (but *forsö'ge* to try), *Fo'rsvar* defence (but *forsva're* to defend, *Forsva'rer* defender). When *for* represents the preposition *for* (Germ. für, vor, Eng. fore) then it has the stress: *Fo'rbön* intercession, *Fo'rbjerg* promuntory, *Fo'rgaard* fore court, *Fo'rhæng* curtain, *Fo'rtand* foretooth, *Fo'rnavn* Christian name, *Fo'rfald* impediment (but *forfa'lden* decayed).

4) words with the negative prefix *u* (Eng. un-, in-) as a rule have the stress on the first syllable; Ex.: *U'naade* disgrace; but adjectives ending in *-elig* and those ending in *-lig* which are derived from verbs and denote a feasibility have the stress on that syllable of the second part of the compound, which had the accent before the composition took place; Ex.: *ubeha'gelig* disagreeable, *umu'lig* impossible, *usaa'rlig* invulnerable, *ugjö'rlig* not feasible. Also a great many other adjectives in *-lig* and *-ig* have the stress on the second part of the compound: *uanstæ'ndig* indecent, *usædva'nlig* unusual, *uhe'ldig* unfortunate, *ua'gtet* although, but *u'farlig* not dangerous, *u'personlig* impersonal, *u'naturlig* unnatural or *unatu'rlig*.

5) The suffixes *-inde* and *-ri* generally have the stress: *Læreri'nde* (lady) teacher, *Generali'nde* general's wife, *Hykleri'* hypocrisy, *Tyveri'* theft, (but *Svi'neri* and *Gri'seri* piggery, filthiness take the stress on the first syllable). The suffixes *-else* and *-ning* usually when added to compound words

cause the accent to be moved forward to the second part of the compound; Ex.: *misʽunde* to envy, but *Misuʽndelse* envy, *Tilvæʽrelse* existence, *Tilskikʽkelse* dispensation (by providence) but *tilʽskikke* to dispense, *Indleʽdning* introduction but *iʽndlede* to introduce); in *Aʽfsættelse* removal, *Uʽdförelse* execution, *Oʽversættelse* translation, *Aʽfledning* derivation, *Uʽdtapning* draining and some others the accent is on the first syllable. Some derivative adjectives with *-lig*, *-ig* (cfr. No. 4) and *-som* have the stress on another syllable than the first (most of these words are of German origin); Ex.: *opriʽgtig* sincere, *ærvæʽrdig* reverend, *forsæʽtlig* intentional (but *Foʽrsæt* intention), *veldæʽdig* charitable, *alvoʽrlig* serious (but *Aʽlvor* earnest).

6) note the following words: *Tallerʽken* plate, *Vidunʽder* miracle, *undtaʽgen* except, *Henseʽende* regard, *vedkomʽmende* in *for mit Vedkomʽmende* as far as I am concerned (but *vedʽkommende* pertaining to).

133. Compound words as a rule have the principal stress on their first part (see § 131); Ex.: *Hoʽvedpine* (pron. *Hoʽdepine*) headache, *Husʽhovmeʼster* majordomus. But in some words the stress is on the second part of the composition:

1) in some titles and geographical names; Ex.: *Oberstlöiʽtnant* lieutenant colonel, *Stiftaʽmtmand* high civil official, *Kristianssaʽnd*, *Frederikshaʽld* (but *Freʽdrikstad*), *Ostinʽdien* East India; furthermore *Sydoʽst* southeast, *Nordveʽst* north west etc. *Velbaaʽrenhed* lordship (and other words composed with *vel-*: *Velgjeʽrning* deed of charity, *Velanstæʽndighed* propriety, *velsmaʽgende* savory, *velsiʽgne* to bless, *Velsiʽgnelse* blessing (but *Velʽlevnet* luxurious living, *Velʽmagt* vigor, *velʽskabt* well shaped etc.), *Skomaʽger* shoemaker, *Budeiʽe* milkmaid, *Smaagutʽter* little boys, *Smaapiʽger* little girls (but *Smaaʽjenter* little girls, has the stress on the first part); some

words composed with *halv* half: *halvanden* one and a half, *halvsjette* five and a half; *Aa'rhundrede* century and *Aa'rtusinde* milennium as a rule have the accent on their first part (aar) but may also have it on the second.

2) compounds the first part of which are prepositions have the stress on the first part when the word as a whole belongs to the same class of words as its second part, but on the second part when this is governed by the preposition; Ex : *O'verhoved* (pron. O'verhode) chief, headman, but *overho'vedet* (pr. overho'de) upon the whole, *tilsjö's* on sea, *tilla'nds* on land, *igaar'* yesterday, *imor'gen* to-morrow, *For'sommer* spring, *For'tid* past tense, but *forti'den* for the time being. Obs. *Efterret'ning* news, but *U'nderretning* or *Underre'tning* information, *forbi'* by, but *fo'rbigaa* to pass by.

des is unstressed when indicating a comparison: *desvæ'rre* the worse, alass, *desme're* the more etc.; but when it represents the old gen. of demonstrative pronoun ruled by the second part of the composition it has the stress: *des'aarsag* on that account, *des'angaaende* thereabout, *des'foruden* moreover besides that (but *desu'den* besides, *desforme'delst* for that reason). *i* in adverbial compounds never has the stress: *imo'd* against, *igje'n* again, *ibla'ndt* among; *saa* is stressed when indicating manner: *saa'lydende* reading as follows, *saa'kaldet* so called; but unstressed when indicating degree: *saasna'rt* as soon, *saafre'mt* provided, *saavi'dt* as far as.

Kanhæ'nde perhaps, *maaske'* (pr. maasje' or maaske') perhaps; but *ka'nske* (pr. ka'nskə or ka'nsjə) perhaps.

134. Different from the stress accent is the musical accent. There are two kinds of musical accent employed in single words, the monosyllabic and the dissyllabic. The former is used in (original) monosyllables and in so far corresponds with the Danish "Stødtone" (Glottal catch), while the dissyllabic accent belongs to (originally) dissyllabic or polysyllabic words.

135. The monosyllabic accent begins in a very low tone and ascends to a somewhat higher pitch, about a third or a fourth. This somewhat higher pitch is the regular base of the voice.

136. The dissyllabic accent begins in a strong medium tone, descends about a third and ascends in the weak final syllable again about a fourth.

[**137.** From professor Johan Storm's "Englische Philologie" are taken the following "tunes" of words with monosyllabic and dissyllabic accent. As many originally monosyllabic words in the present language have two syllables, there will among the words with monosyllabic accent be found many dissyllables.

Eastern Norway (Christiania).
I. Monosyllabic accent.

II. Dissyllabic (compound) accent.

Western Norway (Bergen).
I. Monosyllabic accent. II. Dissyllabic (compound) accent.

(*ja* yes, *Solen* the sun, *Bögerne* the books, *Maanen* the moon, *Menneskene* the human beings)].

138. By their different musical accent are distinguished many pairs of otherwise consonous words. Monosyllabic words with the affixed definite article are, as far as the accent is concerned, considered as monosyllables.

Simple or monosyllabic accent (')	Compound or dissyllabic accent (')
Amen (pron. am'mən), amen.	*Ammen* (pron. am'men) the wet nurse.
Bönder (pr. Bønnər) plasants.	*Bönner* beans (sing. Bønne), *Bönner* prayers (sing. Bøn) pron. Bøn'nər.
Bund-en ('nn) the bottom.	*bunden* ('nn) tied.
Dyr-et (') the animal.	*dyre* expensive (plur.).
Haar-et (haa'ret or haa're(t) the hair).	*haar'et* hairy.
Kok'ken the cook (male, indefinite: *Kok*).	*Kok'ke-n* the cook (woman).
Lom'men the loon (Colymbus arcticus, ind. Lom).	*Lomm-en* (') the pocket.
Sval'-en the balcony.	*Svale-n* the swallow.
Ul(d)en the wool.	*ul(d)en* woolly.
Jæger (name).	*Jæger* hunter.
Möller (name).	*Möller* miller.
(jeg) *bærer* (I) carry, (jeg) *drager* (I) draw.	*Bærer* carrier, (en) *Drager* (a) porter.
(jeg) *lægger* (I) lay.	*Legger* (pr. lægger) calves (of the legs).
(jeg) *löber* (p) (I) run.	*Löber* (p) runner.
(jeg) *læser* (I) read.	*Læser* a reader.
(jeg) *piber* (pipər) (I) pipe.	*Piber* (pipər) pipes.
(jeg) *skriver* (I) write.	*Skriver* penman.
(jeg) *sætter* (I) set.	*Sætter* typesetter.
(jeg) *sæl(g)er* (I) sell.	*Sælger* (g sounded) a seller.

The present tense of the strong verbs have the simple tone, that of the weak verbs the compound tone. The plural form of a great many nouns which in the old language formed their plural in —r still retains the simple tone, while those words which in the old language formed their plural in —ar and —ir have the compound tone.

139. The musical accent of the words may be modified by the sentence or the tonic accent. Thus e. g. a gradual raising of the pitch of the voice through the whole sentence indicates a question or something unfinished, where a continuation of the sentence may be looked for.

ABBREVIATIONS.

140. In colloquial language there are used a great many abbreviations which do not occur in the more solemn language used on the pulpit, in recitals etc.

These abbreviations chiefly consist in the dropping of the syllables *de*, *ge*(ke), *ve*, especially in verbs; most of the words affected by these abbreviations are in some figurative or not very frequent meanings exempt therefrom. Especially may be noticed that the abbreviation as a rule does not take place in pres. partcp. (ending in -*ende*), and before suffixes commencing with -*e*, -*er*, -*en*, -*else* etc.) and in pres. and inf. pass. (ending in -*es*).

a) abbreviations consisting in the omission of *de:*

de dropped.	*de* retained.
be(*de*) to ask, pray, also *be*(*de*) *til Gud* pray to God.	*Bededag* day of prayer, *Tilbedelse* adoration.

de dropped.

blö(d)e to bleed.

bry(de) (in past tense *brydde*) to trouble, *bry sit Hode med* (spelt: bryde sit Hoved) to trouble one's head about something.

bry(de) sig om to mind.

bry(de) en Gut med en Jente to tease a boy about a girl.

by(de) to offer, *by(de) paa noget* to give a bid for something or to invite to partake of something.

fö(de) to bear (give birth) and to feed (especially is the abbreviation the rule in this latter meaning), *sultefö sine Kreaturer* to starve one's cattle.

gli(de) to glide.

glæ(de) to gladden *jeg glæ(de)r mig til de(t)* I anticipate it with pleasure.

klæ(de) to dress, *at klæ(de) paa en* to dress somebody, *det klæ(de)r Dem godt* it fits you well, *Klæ(de)r* clothes, *Haandklæ(de)* towel, *Klæ(de)sbörste* clothes brush.

la(de) et Gevær to load a gun.

la(d) det være let that be, i. e. don't do that (see § 106).

de retained.

mit Hjærte blöder my heart bleeds.

bryde to break (a wholly different word, pres. tense pron. bryte, past tense *bröd* (pron. brøt).

byde command, *Loven byder* the law commands, *sælge til höistbydende* to sell to the highest bidder.

du skal föde en Sön thou shallt bear a son, *Födeland* country of birth. *Födemiddel* aliment.

Glidebane a slide.

Glæde joy, *de(t) glæder mig at höre* I am glad to hear it.

beklæde et Embede to fill an office, *Klæde* cloth, *sort Klæde* black broadcloth, *Ligklæde* pall.

Ladested small town (without a city charter).

lade to leave undone.

de dropped.	*de* retained.
li(de) to suffer, *jeg li(de)r ondt* I suffer hardships.	*lide af en Sygdom* to suffer from a disease, *Lideformen* the passive voice, *lide Skibbrud paa sin Tro* to make shipwreck concerning one's faith.
det li(de)r langt paa Dag it is passing late into the day.	*Tiden lider* time is passing.
ri(de) or *ri(d)e* to ride on horseback, *en Ri(de)tur* a horseback ride.	*Berider* a horse trainer, *Ridekunst* the art of riding.
raa(de) to advise, *Mennesket spaar, Gud raar* man proposes, God disposes.	*forraade* to betray, *tilraade* to counsel, *Omraade* territory, *Raaderum* free scope.
ska(de) to injure, *de(t) kan ikke ska(de)* it can do no harm.	*skade* is the more common form in polite language; *det skader ikke at forsöge* there is no harm done in trying. *af Skade bli(ve)r man klog* injury makes wise.
smede, pron. smi, to forge, *at smi Jern* to forge iron.	*man maa smede, mens Jernet er varmt* you must strike while the iron is hot.
spre(de) to spread, *Epidemien spre(de)r sig over hele Byen* the epidemie spreads all over the town.	*jeg skal sprede mine Fiender* I shall scatter my enemies, *du maa sörge for at adsprede ham* you must take care to divert his thoughts.
stri(de) to strive, *at stri(de) med noget* to strive with something, *at stri(de) imod* to be opposed to.	*det strider mod Fornuften* it is against all reason, *at stride den sidste Strid* to fight the last battle, to die.

de dropped.

træ(de) to step, *at træ(de) en paa Foden* to step on somebody's toes, *træ(d) af* retire!

bety(de) to signify, *hvad bety(de)r dette?* what is the meaning of this?

va(de) to wade.

Bro(de)r brother, *Fa(de)r* father, *Mo(de)r* mother when signifying the degree of relationship; also in compounds: *Farbror* father's brother, *Farfar* father's father, *Farmor, Morfar, Mormor* and *Morbror, Brorskab* (p): *der er intet Brorskap i Kortspil* relationship (brotherhood) is of no avail in cards.

Sadel saddle, pron. Sal in *Sa(de)lmager* a saddler, upholsterer, in other cases usually pronounced *Sale*: *sidde fast i Salen* to have a firm seat.

de retained.

træde i ens Fodspor to follow one's example, *det optræder i Form af* it appears in the shape of; *at tiltræde et Embede* to enter upon an office.

at betyde en noget to give somebody something to understand, *at tyde en Indskrift* to decipher an inscription, *antyde* to intimate, *hentyde* to allude.

Vadefu(g)l wading bird, *Vadested* ford.

Broder, Fader, Moder figuratively: *en Broder i Aanden* a brother in the spirit, *Embedsbroder* a brother officer, *Fostbroder* sworn brother, *Brodermord* fratricide, *Broderkys* brotherly kiss, *broderlig* fraternal, *den hellige Fader* the holy father, *Fadermord* parricide, *Fadermordere* sideboards, *Faderhjærte* paternal heart, *hun er allerede Moder* she is already a mother, *Moderglæde* maternal joy.

b) abbreviations by dropping *ge*.

ge dropped.

dra(ge) to draw, *dra(ge) Pusten* to draw the breath, *dra(ge) Kjendsel paa* to recognize, *dra(ge) en Slutning* to draw a conclusion, *bedra(ge)* to defraud, *jeg har draget* (pr. drad) *ham hele Vejen* I have been dragging him all the way.

si(ge) or *si(g)e* to say, pres. tense always *si(ge)r*, past. *sa(gde)*, imp. *si(g)*, passiv *si(g)es*.

ta(ge) to take, past tense *tog* pron. tok or to, imper. ta, ptcp. *tagen, taget* pron. coloquially tatt.

Morgen pron. mår'n morning, imår'n to-morrow, *imorges* pron. imårres early this morning.

no(ge)n, no(g)en no(g)e(t) anybody, anything.

ge retained.

drage intr. to depart, *med draget Sværd* with drawn sword, *jeg andrager om Udsættelse* I apply for a respite, *Tildragelse* happening (and other derivatives).

sige: 120, siger og skriver et hundrede og tyve 120—say one hundred and twenty—, *efter sigende* according to report, *Frasigelse* resignation (and other derivatives).

tage sometimes in religious diction and always in some derivatives: *Antagelse* supposition, *Fritagelse* exemption, etc.

Morgenstund har Guld i Mund early to rise makes a man wealthy, *Morgenstjerne* (a name).

nogenlunde fairly, *nogensinde* at any time (sometimes pron. någen—).

c) abbreviations by dropping *ve*.

ve dropped.

bli(ve) to become, remain, past tense *ble(v)*, prtcp. *blevet* (pron. blit).

ve retained.

blive in pres. ptcp. and some derivatives.

NORWEGIAN SOUNDS.

ve dropped.	*ve* retained.
fly(ve) or *fly(v)e* to flie, *i fly-(v)ende Fart* in a flying hurry, *paa flyende Flækken* (somewh. vulg.) right here on the spot.	*med flyvende Faner* with banners flying, *den flyvende Hollænder* the flying Dutchman, *en Flyvemaskine* a flying machine, *et Flyveblad* a pamphlet.
gi(ve) to give, *gi(v) mig det* give it me, prtcp. *givet* pr. git (in these abbreviated colloquial forms *g* is pronounced as *j* (see § 118, 2).	*der gives Folk som* there are people who, *anse noget for givet* consider something as given, *en given Störrelse* a given quantity (in the unabridged forms *g* usually is pronounced as *g*).
ha(ve) to have, pres. written and pronounced *jeg har*, past tense spelt *havde* pron. hadde, prtc. *havt* pron hatt.	*havende* having, passive *haves* or *ha(v)es*.
Hoved pron. hode head: *et godt Hode* a clever person, *ondt i Hode(t)* pains in the head, *Hodepine, Hodeverk* headache (always spelt *Hovedpine* etc.)	*Hoved* chief: *Hovedmanden* the head, the leader, *Hovedværk* principal work.

QUANTITY.

141. Vowels are long 1) in monosyllables when ending the word; Ex.: *gaa* to go, *Ko* cow. (*Nu* now has long or short vowel according as it has the sentence stress or not: *nu' kommer jeg* here I am, *nu kom'mer jeg* I am coming now). 2) in the accented syllable of dissyllables and polysyllables when followed by a single consonant with following vowel:

læ·se to read, *Prø·ve* test, *Naa·de* grace. Exceptions: *Abor* perch (pron. abbor), *Furu* fir tree (pron. furru), *Lever* (vv) liver, *Moro* (rr) fun, *Niding* (dd) villain, traitor.

142. Vowels are short when followed by two or more consonants or a double consonant; Ex.: *hoppe* to jump, *mörk* dark, *mange* many.

NOTE 1. Before *st* a vowel may be short or long; Ex.: long: *Bæst* wild beast, *mest* most; short: *Hest* horse, *Vest* waistcoat. If the *t* belongs to an ending of inflection, then a preceding long vowel as a rule retains its length: *hæ·st* hoarse (neut. of hæs), *blæ·st* prtcp. of *blæse* to blow (but *Blœst*, wind), *læ·st* prtc. of *læse* to read; in the same manner a vowel is treated before *l, n, r,* with following inflective *t*: *fø·lte* past tense of *föle* to feel, *gu·lt* yellow, neut. of *gul*, *me·nte* past tense of *mene* to mean, *hö·rt* prtcp. of *hörs* to hear.

NOTE 2. Before *r(d)* the vowel is long (see § 109); Ex.: *Jo·r(d)* earth etc ; but *Sværd* sword, *Hjord* herd with short vowel and pronounced *d*.

NOTE 3. Before *dl, dr, gr, pr* and *tr* the preceding vowel as a rule is long, but may also be short; Ex.: long: *adle* to ennoble, *bedre* better, *magre* lean (plur), *kapre* to capture, (make a prize of). *Theatret* the theater; short: *snadre* to cackle, *pludre* to jabber.

143. In monosyllables ending in a single consonant the vowel may be long or short. It is as a rule long before *b, g, d,* whether they be pronounced as written or as *p, k, t* (or mute d); Ex.: *Haab* hope, *Tog* (å) expedition, *Bad* bath, *Gab* (p) gap, *Tag* (k) roof, *bag* (k) behind, *lad* (t) lazy.

NOTE. Short is the vowel in some words ending in one of the above mentioned consonants (the consonant in that case being pronounced long); Ex.: *Laag* cover, pron. låkk (but *Öjenlaag* eyelid as written), *Leg*, gg, leg, *Væg*, gg, wall, *Ryg*, gg, back, *tig*, gg, imper. of *tigge* to beg, *lig*, gg, imper. of *ligge* to lie, *Lab*, bb, paw, *Flab*, bb, chaps.

144. A vowel followed by a single *l, n, r, s,* may be long or short, the consonant in the latter case being pronounced long; Ex.: *Hul*, ll, hole, but *hu·l* hollow, *for*, rr, for, but *fo·r* travelled, *vis*, ss, certain, but *vi·s* wise, *Me·n* injury, but *men*, nn, but; a vowel followed by a single *m* is short except in *E·m* vapor.

145. A vowel before a single final *k*, *p*, *t* as a rule is short, the consonant then being pronounced long; Ex.: *Tak*, kk, thanks, *Hop*, pp, jump, *Hat*, tt, hat.

Exceptions are some specific N o r w e g i a n words which have never been accepted into the Danish literature and therefore never have been spelled in accordance with Danish pronunciation: *Aat* food of fishes, *Laat* sound (=Danish *Lyd*), *laak* (being) in poor healt, *Raak* a lane of water through the ice, *Löp* a kind of wooden box.

NOTE. In compound words the component parts retain their original quantity; Ex.: *Tog-tabel* a Railroad time table, *Mod-stand* (pr. Motstand) opposition.

146. A consonant is always long after a stressed short vowel; when an unstressed vowel follows then the consonant is written double; *Hul* hole, plur. *Huller*, *Suppe* soup, *Smör* butter (*Smörret* the butter).

NOTE 1. It will be seen from the above examples that if during the inflection of words ending in a single consonant with a preceding short vowel the consonant comes before a termination commencing in a vowel then the consonant is written double.

NOTE 2. Some foreign words retain their original spelling but are pronounced in accordance with the above rule; Ex.: *Artikel* (pr. artikkel) article, *Amen* (pr. Ammen), *Titel* (pr. Tittel) title. A consonant written double after an unstressed vowel is pronounced short; Ex.: *Tallerken* (pr. Tale'rken) plate, *Parallel* (pr. Parale'll).

NOTE 3. A consonant is not written double before another consonant even if it be long; Ex.: *gammel* old, plur. *gamle* (pr. gammle); except in compound words: Ex.: *Manddrab* homicide (Mand-drab). A long consonant is not as a rule written double at the end of words, except in a few cases to avoid ambiguity; Ex.: *viss* certain, to distinguish it from *vi·s* wise.

VOWEL CHANGES IN INFLECTION AND WORD FORMATION.

147. The Dano-Norwegian language employs two most important kinds of vowel changes, which the Danish and Norwegian grammarians call "*Aflyd*" and "*Omlyd*", in English generally called "gradation" and "mutation".

148. By g r a d a t i o n (Aflyd, ablaut) we understand that system of the language enabling it out of the same root to form several stems by using different vowels; this principle is of great importance in the inflection of the verbs, but it also plays an important part in word formation; Ex.: *bære* to bear, *bar* bore, *baaren* borne, *binde* to bind, *bandt* bound, *Baand* ribbon, *Bundt* bunch, *tage* take, *tog* took.

149. By m u t a t i o n (Omlyd, umlaut) is understood the change of a vowel caused by assimilation to a following vowel (*i*, *u*) or consonant (*j*). The sound causing the change has in the present language as a rule disappeared, but it is shown by a comparison with the earlier stages of the language. The principle of mutation is active both in inflection and in word formation. The u-umlaut is now in inflection found only in the word *Barn* child, plur. *Börn*.

By the i-umlaut the following changes are caused:

a—æ: *Fader* father, plur. *Fædre*, *falde* to fall, *fælde* to fell.
aa—æ: *Haand* hand, plur. *Hænder*.
o—ø: *Moder* mother, plur. *Mødre*, *Blod* blood, *bløde* to bleed.
u—y: *tung* heavy, comp. *tyngre*, *huld* gracious, *hylde* to swear allegiance to.

NOTE. In the i-umlaut it is a following front sound that influences (palatalizes) a preceding back sound.

ETYMOLOGY.

ARTICLES.—GENDERS.

150. The Dano-Norwegian language has a definite and an indefinite article. The definite article has two forms, one employed in connection with a noun alone, the other used with a noun qualified by an adjective or with an adjective alone. The former is called the post-positive article (also the definite article of the substantives). The latter is called the præ-positive article (also the definite article of the adjectives).

151. The Dano-Norwegian language has two genders, c o m m o n gender and n e u t e r. The former comprises both the masculine and feminine of the old language.

NOTE. In colloquial Norwegian speech there is still sometimes made a distinction between the masculine and feminine genders. The cases where such distinction is made will be mentioned in their proper places.

152. The post-positive article is:

common gender.	neuter.	plural.
-en (-n)	-et (-t)	-ne (-ene).
gen. -ens	-ets	-nes (-enes).

Ex.: *Hest-en* the horse, *Hus-et* the house, *Huse-ne* the houses, *Mængde-n* the quantity, *Værelse-t* the room, *Mænd-ene* the men. Thus it appears that the forms -*n*, -*t* are used in connection with nouns ending in -*e* and the form *ene* in connection with words forming their plural without an ending.

NOTE 1. This article was originally a demonstrative pronoun which in the old language has the form of *hinn*, *hitt*, *hinir* and by being used enclitically with nouns gradually lost its independent character and a part of its substance. This enclitic definite article is one of the chief characteristics distinguishing the Scandinavian languages from the other Teutonic tongues.

NOTE 2. The enclitic (post-positive) article, besides being used with substantives standing alone, is employed with substantives qualified by the following adjectives: *al* all, *begge* both, *selv* self; Ex.: *al Maden* all the food, *selve Kongen* or *Kongen selv* the king himself, *begge Brödrene* both the brothers.

153. The præ-positive definite article is:

  comm. gender. neuter.   plural.
   den   *de(t)*   *de*

den store Man(d) the great man, *de(t) nye Hus* the new house; plur.: *de store Mænd* the great men. This article may also be employed with an adjective alone when used substantively: *den gode* the good (man), *de(t) skjönne* the beautiful, beauty.

NOTE 1. With the following adjectives the postpositive and the præpositive article may be used promiscuously: *hel* whole, *halv* half; Ex.: *hele Dagen* or *den hele Dag* the whole day, *halve Riget* or *det halve Rige* half the kingdom, *største, mindste Delen* the greater, smaller part. Sometimes, mostly in poetry, the postpositive article may be used where the præpositive is regularly employed: *et Skud af gamle Heltestammen* a scion of the old stock of heroes, *Svenske Kysten* or *den svenske Kyst* the Swedish coast.

NOTE 2 Colloquially it is common in Norway to use both the post-positive and the præ-positive article at the same time with nouns qualified by an adjective; Ex.: *den store Manden* the big man. In the same manner the postpositive article is in Norwegian often added to nouns determined by demonstrative pronouns: *i denne Villaen* in this villa here; *den Manden der* that man there. This is not used in Danish.

NOTE 3. The præpositive article is sometimes in poetry and religious style used with nouns not qualified by adjectives; Ex: *Brevet til de Romere* the Epistle to the Romans, *de Vover saa sagtelig trille* the waves roll leisurely along.

NOTE 4. The præpositive article is originally the same word as the demonstrative pronoun *den, det, de* which has lost its logical stress and consequently its accent stress and has come to be considered as a mere prefix.

154. Some words are in Danish used without an article, while the English language requires the article with the same words; Ex.: *Verden* the world, *Verden er stor* the world is great (but *i Kunstverdenen* in the world of art), *Höjesteret* the Supreme Court, *Rektor* the Principal (of the School).

Furthermore may be noted that the article is never affixed to a noun that is qualified by a genitive: *Kongens Slot* the palace of the king, *Naboens Hus* the house of the neighbor. But if a complement (*af* of, with a noun) is used instead of genitive, then the article is used: *Ejeren af Huset* or *Husets Ejer* the owner of the house.

Sometimes the præpositive article may be omitted with superlatives: *förste Gang* the first time, *överste Stokværk* the top floor, *med störste Fornöjelse* with the greatest pleasure. But in all these cases the article may also be used.

155. The indefinite article has the form:

common gender.   neuter.
    en   *et*

Ex.: *en Man(d)* a man, *et Hus* a house.

NOTE 1. The indefinite article was originally the numeral *en* one.

NOTE 2. The indefinite article always has its place before the noun and also before a qualifying adjective: *en Mand, en stor Mand*. But when the noun is connected with an interrogative word or an adjective qualified by the adverb *saa* so, and *for* too, then the article is placed after the interrogative word, or adjective; Ex.: *hvilken en Mand* what a man? *hvor stort et Hus* what a big house! *saa ungt et Menneske* such a youth! *for tyk en Hals* too thick a neck. In connection with *mangen* the article has its place after that word but before another adjective: *mangen en Mand* many a man, *mangen en tapper Mand* many a brave man. In connection with *saadan* such, the article may be placed before or after that word: *saadan en Mand* or *en saadan Mand*. In connection with a comparative and *jo—desto* the article is placed between the comparative and the noun; Ex.: *jo tykkere en Hals han har, desto snarere skal den hugges over* the thicker a neck he has, the quicker he shall be decapitated. (In this case the article is more commonly omitted).

NOTE 3. The indefinite article is used in connection with numerals to indicate an approximate number; Ex.: H*r. Sörensen var her i fjorten Dage* Mr. S. stayed here about two weeks.

NOUNS.

GENDER OF THE NOUNS.

156. The genders of the nouns are only of importance syntactically, in so far as the adjective or the article assume different forms in conformity with the gender of the noun qualified by them. No generally binding rules can be given for the genders of the nouns in Danish-Norwegian, but the following intimations may be of some help:

1) Most words denoting living beings are of common gender. *En Mand* a man, *en Hest* a horse, *en Hund* a dog, *en Ko* a cow, *en Flue* a fly.

NOTE 1. Some nouns comprising the natural masculine and feminine genders are neuter: *Kvæget*, the cattle; *Folket* the people (also the compounds: *et Mandfolk, et Kvindfolk* a male, female individual), *Mennesket* man (generally), *et Dyr* an animal, *et Svin* a hog, *et Faar* a sheep, *et Æsel* a donkey. Also several words indicating the young ones of animals: *et Lam* a lamb, *et Føl* a colt, *et Kid* a kid.

2) Names of t r e e s, p l a n t s and s t o n e s are as a rule of common gender: *Bøgen* the beech, *en Eg* an oak, *Rugen* the rye, *Graniten* the granite, *Flinten* the flint.

NOTE 2. Neuter are: *et Blad* a leaf, *et Bær* a berry; (but in compounds common gender in Norwegian when used collectively; Ex.:

ETYMOLOGY. 71

Multebæren staar röd over hele Myren the cloudberry stands red all over the bog), *et Græs* a grass, *et Straa* a straw, *et Træ* a tree.

3) Names of s e a s o n s, m o n t h s, d a y s and other d i v i- s i o n s o f t i m e are mostly common gender. *Hösten* the fall, *Vinteren* the winter, *Dagen* the day.

NOTE 3. *Aaret* the year, *et Dögn* day & night, *et Minut* a minute (but *paa Minuten* this very minute).

4) Names of w i n d and w e a t h e r: *Östenvinden* the East wind, *Sneen* the snow, *Stormen* the storm. (But *Hagl* hail, may be c. and n. and *Regn* rain is in Norway usually n., *Vejret* the weather).

5) Names of r i v e r s and l a k e s: *den blaa Donau* the blue D., *Rhinen* the Rhine, *den grönne Gjendin* the green G.

6) Names of sciences: *Filologien, Medicinen, Mathematiken.*

157. 1) Most collective nouns and names of substances are of neuter gender: *Træet* the wood, *Blyet* the lead, *Jernet* the iron, *Staalet* the steel. But *Malmen* the ore, *Ulden* the wool, *Melken* the milk, *Vinen* the wine, and others.

2) Names af c o u n t r i e s and c i t i e s: *det lille Danmark* the little Denmark, *det mægtige Rom* the mighty R.

3) Names of m o u n t a i n s: *det höje Mont Blanc* the high M. B., *det ildsprudende Ætna* the fire spouting Æ.

NOTE. Names of letters are in Denmark usually of neuter, in Norway of common gender: *et stort* (Nor. *en stor*) A a capital A. Also in Denmark *et Bogstav* a letter, i Norway *en Bogstav*. Names of languages are of common gender when combined with the post-positive article. *Fransken* the French language, *Græsken* Greek; but *paa godt Norsk* in good Norwegian.

158. The following nominal suffixes form words af common gender: 1) *-hed, -inde, -ing, (-ling, -ning) -er* (nomina agentis), *-en* (nomina actionis), *-ske, -dom*; Ex.: *Storhed* greatness, *Lærerinde* (lady) teacher, *Stilling* position, *Virkning* effect, *Gjæsling* gosling, *Beiler* suitor, *Vaklen* vacillation, *Barndom* childhood.

2) as a rule *-sel*, *-else*, *-e* (in derivatives of adjectives), *-d*, *-t*, *-st*,; *Færdsel* traffic (but *et Fængsel* prison, *et Stængsel* bar, *et Bidsel* a bit, bridle), *Förelse* guidance (but *et Spögelse* a ghost, *et Værelse* a room), *Styrke* strenght, *Höjde* height, (but *Mörket* the darkness), *Byrd* birth, *Færd* behavior, *Kunst* art, *Magt* power (but *et Skridt* a step).

3) Foreign words ending in *-ion*, *-isme*, *-tet*, *-ur*, *-us*: *Kommunionen*, *Radikalismen*, *en Kalamitet* (but *Universitetet*), *en Kultus*, *en Habitus*, *Kulturen* (but *et Kreatur*); *Diktatur* may be used both as c. and n.

159. 1) Nouns having the same form as the stem of verbs are usually neuter; Ex.: *Badet* the bath (*bade* to bathe), *Kaldet* the call (*kalde* to call), *Raabet* the cry (*raabe* to cry).

NOTE. This rule does not apply in cases where the verb is derived from the corresponding noun (although, of course, also in that case the noun may be neuter); thus we have *en Dröm* a dream (*at drömme* to dream), *en Leg* a play (*at lege* to play), *Trösten* the comfort (*at tröste* to comfort). Also *Drik* drink, *Grav* grave, *Hjælp* help, *Straf* punishment, *Strid* strife, *Törst* thirst are common gender, and so are words ending in *-gt* as *Frygten* the fright (*at frygte* to fear), and those in *-ang*, to which correspond verbs in *-inge* (*ynge*), *Sangen* the song (*at synge* to sing), *Klangen* the sound (*at klinge* to sound).

2) The following suffixes as a rule form words of neuter gender: *-dömme*, *-ende*, *-maal*, *-ri*, *-skab*; *med mit Vidende* with my knowledge, (but *i en Henseende* in one respect, *denne Tidende* this news, *en Tiende* a tithe), *Kongedömmet* the kingdom, *et Spörgsmaal* a question, *Tyveriet* the theft, *Bageriet* baker's shop, *mit Kjendskab* my knowledge, *Ægteskabet* marriage (but derivatives of adjectives are of common gender: *Troskaben* the faithfulness, *Ondskaben* the wickedness).

3) Foreign words ending in *-iv, -ment, -om, -um* are neuter; *et Komplement* (but *en Kompliment*); *et Ultimatum, et Arkiv, et Axiom.*

160. Compound words have the gender of the last component part: *en Bordplade* a table slab, *et Hesteben* a horse's leg.

Exceptions: *En Ödeland* a spendthrift, *en Graaskjæg* a greybeard, *et Folkefærd* a race, *et Gjenfærd* a ghost, *et Vidnesbyrd* a testimony, *dette Perlemo(de)r* this mother-of-pearl, *Brændevinet* the brandy, *Forskjellen* the difference (but *Grændseskjellet* the border line).

161. Some words imply a different meaning according as they are used in common gender or neuter. In other cases originally different words have the same sound, but disagree in gender.

common gender	neuter
Arken the ark.	*et Ark* a sheet (of paper).
en Bid (Norw. *Bit, Bete*) a bit, piece.	*et Bid* (dd) a bite.
en Bo (in compounds *Nabo* etc. a neighbor).	*et Bo* an estate.
en Brug a custom.	*et Brug* (Norw.) establishment, concern.
en Buk a he-goat.	*et Buk* a bow.
Felten the campaign.	*Feltet* the field, sphere.
en Frö a frog.	*et Frö* a seed.
en Fyr a fellow, chap.	*et Fyr* a light-house.
en Fölge a consequence.	*et Fölge* a retinue.
Lejen the rent.	*Lejet* the couch.
en Lem a trap.	*et Lem* a member.
en Lod share, lot.	*et Lod* a weight.
en Nögle a key.	*et Nögle* (D.) a ball (of yarn)
en Raad (in compounds: *Statsraad,* etc.) a councillor.	*et Raad* a council, advice.

common gender	neuter
Rimen the hoar frost.	*Rimet* the rhyme.
Risen the rice.	*Riset* the fagots, rod.
en Segl (D.) a sickle.	*et Segl* a seal (also *et Sejl* a sail).
en Skrift a (hand) writing.	*et Skrift* a writing, a book.
en Spand (D., *et Spand* N.) a pail.	*et Spand* a span, a team.
en Stift a tack.	*et Stift* a diocese.
en Söm a seam.	*et Söm* (D., *en Söm* N.) a nail.
en Ting a thing.	*et Thing* (*Ting*) assembly.
en Tryk a print.	*et Tryk* (N. also *et T.*) a pressure.
en Træk a draught (of air).	*et Træk* a feature.
Vaaren the spring.	*et Vaar* (D., N. *et Var*) a cover.
en Værge a guardian.	*et Værge* a weapon.
en Væv a tissue.	*noget Væv* nonsense.
Vælde power (*i al sin Vælde* in all his might).	*Vælde* (N. in compounds *Enevældet* the absolute monarchy; D. *Enevælden*).
en Æsel (D., *et Æ.* N.) an ass.	*et Æsel* a donkey.

In some words the gender is not quite fixed, so they sometimes appear as neuter, at other times as of common gender. Ex.: *Fond* (D. *en* and *et*, N. always *et*) fund, *Helbred* (D., always c. N.) health, *Katalog* (D., always c. N.) catalogue, *Lak* (D. c. and n., No. always n.) sealing wax, *Lög* (D. always c. N.) onion; *Tarv* requirements. Sometimes the gender differs in Danish and Norwegian, as can be seen from some of the examples given above; *Kontingent* is in D. n., in N. c. *Kind* cheek, D. c., N. mostly n.

162. Something different from the question of grammatical gender is the circumstance that the language in some cases has different words to denote the natural genders. Thus the genders can be distinguished:

1) by adding the feminine ending *-inde* to the masculine word: *Greve* count—*Grevinde* countess; *Lærer* teacher—*Lærerinde* female teacher; *Löve* lion—*Lövinde* lioness;

2) by adding the feminine ending *-ske* to the masculine word: *Opvarter* waiter—*Opvarterske* waitress (usually *Opvartningsjomfruen*); *Berider* riding-master, circus-rider—*Beriderske* female rider.

NOTE. The ending *-ske* is usually applied to denote persons of lower position than *-inde*, but sometimes both may be used: *Sangerinde* and *Sangerske* (less common) songstress.

3) by adding the words *-kone* woman, *-pige* girl, *-jomfru* miss to the masculine words or to the corresponding verbs: *Vaskerkonen*, *Vaskerpigen* the laundress, *Badekonen*, *Badejomfruen* the woman attendant (at the bath), but *Badetjeneren* the man attendant.

4) in some foreign words the foreign feminine endings are retained: *Baronesse*, *Comtesse*, *Prinsesse*, *Restauratrice* woman restaurant keeper.

5) The two natural genders of animals are usually denoted by *Han* he and *Hun* she placed before the name: *Hanbjörn*, *Hunbjörn* (N. *Bingse*, *Binne*) he-bear, she-bear *Hankat*, *Hunkat* (N. *Kjœtte*) tom-cat, tib-cat. But in some cases there are different words for the two genders Ex.: *Buk*—*Gjed* he-goat, she-goat, *Væder*—*Faar* (N. *Sau*) ram—sheep, ewe.

INFLECTION OF NOUNS.

162b. The nouns of the Danish and Dano-Norwegian language have two cases and two numbers. The cases are: nominative and possessive (genitive).

163. **The formation of the possessive.** The possessive is formed by adding -s to the nominative (but w i t h o u t apostrophe).

	S.	Pl.
Nom.	Mand	Mænd.
Poss.	Mands	Mænds.

When the noun has the postpositive definite article, the *–s* is added to the latter:

Nom.	Manden	Mændene	Huset	Husene.
Poss.	Mandens	Mændenes	Husets	Husenes.

NOTE 1. Nouns ending in *s* (*z*, *x*) form their possessive by adding *es;* Ex.: *den lille Gaases Mening* the opinion of that little goos. *Paradises rindende Kilde* the running fountain of Paradise; *paa et forgyldt Paladses flade Tag* on the flat roof of a guilt palace. But as a rule the possessive form of these words, except in the definite form, is avoided. Proper nouns ending in —*s* may have their possessive of same form as the nominative, only adding an apostrophe, or an *s* with preceding a p o s t r o p h e may be added. Ex.: *Sokrates'* of Socrates, *Valders's Fjelddale* the mountain valleys of Valders. Biblical nouns are sometimes used with the Latin gen. form: *Mose Lov* Moses' law, *Pauli Breve* St. Paul's epistles.

NOTE 2. A prepositional complement following the noun which it determines is considered as one word with it and the possessive *s* is added to the complement: *Kongen af Danmarks Brystsukker* the king of Denmarks barley sugar (a kind of cough drops), *Keiseren over alle Russeres Rige* the realm of the Emperor of all Russians.

When several nouns are used to denote one person or thing only the last word gets the *s*: *Kong Olavs Hoer* the army of king O.

NOTE 3 Some names of cities, especially those ending in a vowel, have their possessive (when employed as definitive genitive) like the nominative: *Kristiania By, Kristiania Universitet* etc. the city of Ch., the university of Ch., but *Kristianias Indbyggere* the inhabitants of Ch. In the same manner: *Hamar Stift* the diocese of H., *Kallundborg By, Sorö Academi, Aalborg Skole* the school of Aa., *Kongsberg Sölvværk* the silver mines of K. (but *Bergens By, Trondhjems Domkirke* the Cathedral of T. *Kjöbenhavns Universitet* the university of Copenhagen).

Note 4. In the old language the possessive *s* was added both to the article and the noun; Ex : *land,* gen. *landsins.* A rest of this mode of inflection is found in such expressions as: *Landsens Kost* a country bill of fare, *Livsens Træ* the tree of life, *du er Dödsens* you are a dead man. Also such forms as: *Hjærtens Lyst* the desire of the heart, *Alterens Sakramente* the Lord's supper, find their explanation in the old language where the genitive of the definite article neuter had the form of i n s (or n s), not *ets* (*ts*) as now. A rest of an old genitive plur. is found in such expressions as: *tilhaande (gaa en tilhaande* to assist one); *tilgrunde* to the bottom, *tilgode* due, *tilfulde* fully, *tilbage* back,(O. N. *til handa* to the hands etc).

164. Syntactical remarks about the use of the possessive. The possessive is employed to convey the meaning of possessive, subjective, objective and definitive genitive. In stead of the possessive may in some meanings be used a complement with *af* (or colloquially *til*). *Han er Sön af sin Fader* and *han er sin Faders Sön* he is a son of his father, *Hunden til Pedersen* and *Pedersens Hund* P's dog. The possessive meaning i. e. the pure relation of property can, different from English, never be expressed by *af*. If two kinds of genitive (poss. and obj. or subj. and obj.) occur in connection with one word, then the objective genitive must be expressed by *af*. Thus it is wrong to say: *Hr. Pedersens Afstraffelse af Hr. Kristensen* to indicate the punishment of Mr P. by Mr. K.; it means Mr. P's punishment of Mr. K.

A peculiar use of the possessive form is to express a past time in such expressions as: *igaaraftes* last night, *iaftes* last night (but *iaften* this night); *iforgaars* the day before yesterday, *ihöstes* last fall, *ivaares* last spring.

The possessive form is very common as the first part of compound words: *Landsmand* countryman, *Krigsskib* warship, *skadeslös* indemnified (probably analogously with this latter word are formed the following with irregular genitive in -*es: frugtes-*

lös fruitless, *magteslös*, *krafteslös* powerless, *stundeslös* fidgety, *trösteslös* disconsolate). The genitive is especially frequently used when the first part of the composition is itself a compound word: *Kirketaarnsur* a church steeple clock (but *Taarnur* a tower clock): *Sandstensmur* a sand stone wall (but *Stenmur* a stone wall)Such possessives may sometimes be found as first part of a composition even if there is no corresponding nominative; Ex.: *Fralandsvind* a land breeze (*Vinden staar fra Land* the breeze sets from land).

NOTE: Neither possessive nor *af* is used to connect a name of material to a name of measure: *et Glas Öl* a glass of beer, *en Fluske Vin* a bottle of wine, *en Tönde Poteter* a barrel of potatoes etc.

165. Remains of an old gen. plur. are found in a great many compound words the first part of which ends in *e* (O. N. *a*). *Sengested* bedstead, *Stoleben* chair's leg, *Barneaar* years of childhood (*Börnebal* childrens ball, *Börnehave* kindergarten are exclusively Danish, in N. they say — or are taught to say — *Barnebal, Barnehave*).

166. Remains of an old dative is found in the adverbial phrases: *ad Aare* next year, *itide* in due time, *ilive* alive, *paafærde* abroad, at work, *iyjære* in progress, etc.

THE FORMATION OF THE PLURAL.

---

167. The plural is formed in the following manners:

I) by adding *r* or *er* to the singular, with or without "mutation" (see § 149).

II) by adding *e* to the singular, in a few cases with "mutation."

III) the plural has the same form as the singular, except that in a few cases the vowel is changed by "mutation".

168. First Declension.

Paradigms: *Flaade* fleet, *Rige* empire, *Tand* tooth, *Konsul*, *Kjedel* kettle:

	Indef. Sing.	Def. Sing.	Indef. Plur.	Def. Plur.
N.	Flaade	Flaaden	Flaader	Flaaderne.
Poss.	Flaades	Flaadens	Flaaders	Flaadernes.
N.	Rige	Riget	Riger	Rigerne
Poss.	Riges	Rigets	Rigers	Rigernes.
N.	Tand	Tanden	Tænder	Tænderne.
Poss.	Tands	Tandens	Tænders	Tændernes.
N.	Konsul	Konsulen	Konsuler	Konsulerne.
Poss.	Konsuls	Konsulens	Konsulers	Konsulernes.
N.	Kjedel	Kjedlen	Kjedler	Kjedlerne.
Poss.	Kjedels	Kjedlens	Kjedlers	Kjedlernes.

Remarks. 1) Words ending in an unaccented –e add –r. Exceptions: *Öie* eye, has plural *Öine*; *Tilfælde* case, and *Öre* a coin have plural the same as singular. Antiquated is *Ören* plur. of *Öre* ear, and *Öksne* (*Öxne*) plur. of *Okse* (*Oxe*); *Menneske* man (generally) has plur. *Mennesker* but def. form *Menneskene*, *Bonde* peasant forms it plural with "mutation": *Bónder*.

2). Words ending in stressed vowel (or an unaccented vowel that is not *e*) add –er: *Toga* –*Togaer*; *Mo* heath *Moer*. Except.: *Sko* shoe plur. same as sing.

3) The following monosyllables form their plural with –e r and "mutation".

And duck; *Mark* a weight (½ lb. also unchanged in plural); *Rand* border, *Stand* state, (condition of life), *Stang* pole, *Tang* thongs, *Haand* hand, *Stad* city, *Kraft* power. (Plural: *Ænder* (N.) *Mærker*, *Rænder*, *Stænder*, *Stænger*, *Tænger*, *Hænder*, *Stæder*, *Kræfter*). N. *Skaak* shaft (of a sleigh) plur. *Skjæker.* *Bod* fine, plur. *Böder*; *Fod* foot, pl. *Födder*; *Rod* root, pl. *Rödder*; *Bog* book, pl. *Böger*; N. *Glo(d)* live coal, pl. *Glöder* (or *Glör*); N. *Not* seine, plur. *Nöter.* *Raa* yard (ship's), *Taa* toe, *Klo* claw, have their pl. D. *Ræer*, *Tæer*, *Klöer* (se § 17); N. *Rær*, *Tær*, *Klör*. *Ko* cow, D. pl. *Kjöer* or *Köer* (se § 17). N. *Kjör* (Def. *Kjörne* or N. *Kjörene*).

Most of these words, in spite of consisting in plural of two syllables, have the monosyllabic accent (see §§ D. 76, N. 134).

4) A great many monosyllables of common gender form their plural in *-er* without mutation: Ex.: *Aander* spirits, *Sager* cases, *Floder* rivers, and with doubling of final consonant: *Sönner* sons, *Knapper* buttons; and N. *Gutter* boys.

In some words the Danish and the Norwegian forms of the language disagree: *Plads* place, D. *Pladser*, N. *Pladse*.

Also the following neuter monnosyllables form their plural in *-er*: *Bryst* breast, *Gods* estate, *Hul* hole, *Lem* member, *Loft* ceiling, *Punkt* point, *Skjört* skirt, *Syn* sight, *Værk* work; so also the polysyllables: *Bryllup* wedding, *Hoved* head, *Herred* township, *Hundred*, *Tusind* thousand, *Lærred* linen, *Linned* linen, *Marked* fair.

5) Words ending in −e l, e n, −i n g, −h e d, −s k a b and derivative −s t (*t*) and *d*: *Gjæster* guests, *Kunster* arts, *Togter* expeditions, *Bygder* settlements. Words ending in −e l and some ending in −e n drop their e before the ending: *Kjedel* kettle, *Kjedler*, *Lagen* (bed)sheet, *Lagner* or *Lagener*.

In the same manner: *Foged* sheriff, plur. *Fogder*.

NOTE: *Olding* old man, *Slægtning* kinsman, *Yngling* young man as a rule form their plural in *-e*, but may also take *-er*: *Engel* angel, *Djævel* devil, *Himmel* heaven form their plural by adding *-e* and dropping the *e* of their second syllable: *Engle*, *Djævle*, *Himle* (see § 109).

6) Most foreign words add −e r: *Konsuler*, *Patriarker*, *Prindser* etc. But *Vest* plur. *Veste*. Foreign words ending in *um* drop their *um* before −*er*: *Verbum—Verber*. But *Album—Albums* or *Albumer*. *Pretiosum—Pretiosa*.

Also proper nouns used in plural to denote several persons of same name. Ex.: *Hedviger*, *Örstederne* but *Öhlenschlägere*. Furthermore other classes of words (not adjectives) used substantively: *Jaerne og Neierne* the yeas and noes.

169. Second Declension.

Paradigms: *Stol* chair, *Hat* hat, *Fader* father.

	Indef. Sing.	Def. Sing.	Indef. Plur.	Def. Plur.
N.	Stol	Stolen	Stole	Stolene.
P.	Stols	Stolens	Stoles	Stolenes.
N.	Hat	Hatten	Hatte	Hattene.
P.	Hats	Hattens	Hattes	Hattenes.
N.	Fa(de)r	Fa(de)ren	Fædre	Fædrene.
P.	Fa(de)rs	Fa(de)rens	Fædres	Fædrenes.

Most monosyllables of common gender ending in a consonant follow this declension. Also words ending in −e r irrespective of gender; some of these drop the *e* of their last syllable before the *e* of the ending: *Ager* field, plural *Agre; Fingre* fingers, *Skuldre* shoulders.

But most words ending in −e r retain the *e* of the second syllable in plural: *Ankere* anchors, *Bægere* cups, *Undere* wonders. Especially all nouns denoting persons belonging to a trade or nationality or engaged in an occupation, ending in −e r: *Bagere* bakers, *Sangere* singers, *Tyskere* Germans. Words ending in plural in −*ere* drop their last *e* before the article: *Bægere—Bægerne*.

NOTE. In Denmark they say: *en Dansker*, pl. *Danskerne*, a Dane, and *en Svensker*, pl. *Svenskerne*, a Swede.

In Norway they say: *en Danske*, plur. *Dansker*, and *en Svenske*, plur. *Svensker*.

The following words form their plural in *-e* with "mutation": *Bro(d)er* brother, *Brödre*; *Moder* mother, *Mödre*; *Fader* father, *Fædre*; *Datter* daughter, *Dötre*.

NOTE 2. Colloquially it is common in Norway to give those words of common gender, which in the literary language take plural *-e*, the ending *-e r*: *Hester*, *Hunder*, *Hatter* etc. Also the neuters *Huser*, *Gulver* etc., but most neuters are unchanged in plural; Ex.: *Bord* table, *Tag* roof. Before the article *-n e* the *r* is dropped in the pronunciation, so they say: *Hestene*, *Hattene*, *Guttene* etc. *Broder* etc. never add *-e r*.

170. Third Declension.

Paradigm: *Ord* word.

N.	*Ord*	*Ordet*	*Ord*	*Ordene.*
P.	*Ords*	*Ordets*	*Ords*	*Ordenes.*

Most neuters ending in a consonant follow this declension. Exceptions: *Bord* table, *Brev* letter, *Gulv* floor, *Hus* house, *Navn* name, *Skib* ship, *Sogn* parish, *Tag* roof, *Toug* (N. *Taug*) rope and some others take *-e*: *Borde* etc.; others take *-e r* (see § 165, 4 and 5, and § 169 note 2.) "Mutation" without any ending have: *Mand* man, plur. *Mænd*; *Gaas* goose, plur. *Gjæs* (D. also *Gæs*) *Barn* child has plural *Börn* and *Barnebarn* grandchild pl. *Börneborn*. These are the only remains of the U-mutation of the old language. In Norway they say (and have commenced to write): pl. *Barn* and *Barnebarn* (the same as singular).

171. Some nouns have regularly no plural on account of their signification. Such are proper and collective nouns, names of substances, and abstract nouns indicating a quality. Ex.: *Björnson*, *Jern* iron, *Godhed* goodness. So also words, which otherwise take a plural, when they are used collectively. Ex.: *Har du faaet meget Fisk* (or *mange Fisk*) *idag* have you caught many fish to-day. Words indicating measures or values when ending in a consonant have, as a rule, in that meaning and when connected with a numeral, no plural. Ex.: *To Fod Vand* two feet of water (but *to Födder* two feet, as part of the body). Other such words: *Alen* ell, *Meter*, *Fad* cask, *Anker* anker, *Daler* Dollar, *Glas* glass. But *Krone* crown (coin), *Tönde* barrel, and others ending in –e take plural; also *Pot* (*Potte*) quart, *Oksehoved* hog's head, plur. *Oksehoveder*, *Mark* (½ lb) may have plur. N. *Mærker*, but also unchanged, *Bog* quire, plur. *Böger*, *Favn* cord and fathom pl. *Favne*. *Læst*, last (two Reg. tons) pl. *Læster*. Also: *en Hær paa 1000 Mand* an army of 1000 men.

Other nouns only occur in plural; Ex.: *Forældre* parents, *Forfædre* ancestors, *Söskende* brothers and sisters (at least one of each), *Penge* money, *Indvolde* entrails, *Briller* eyeglasses, *Tyvekoster* (also *Koster* alone) stolen property, *Höns* chickens.

Others have singular but in a different meaning from the plural: *Klæder* clothes, but *Klæde* cloth (see also § 140), *Kopper* (*Smaakopper*) smallpox, but *Kop—Kopper* cup, *Midler* means (money), *Middel* means (instrument).

NOTE: Colloquially it is common to say: *Jeg er gode Venner med ham* I am on friendly terms with him.

THE ADJECTIVES.

I. Declension of Adjectives.

172. The adjectives have a **strong** or **indefinite** and a **weak** or **definite** form.

173. The indefinite form has its neuter ending in *t*, its plural in –*e*. The definite form has the ending –*e* all through

Paradigm: *lang* long.

	c. g.	neut.	plur.
Indefinite	lang	langt	lange.
Definite	lange	lange	lange.

NOTE. The definite form of the adjective may be used as a substantive and may then take the possessive ending *-s*; Ex.: *De fattiges Glæder er(e) af en anden Art end de riges* the pleasures of the poor are of another kind than those of the rich.

NOTE 2. A remnant of an old accusative singular m is found in poetical language: *paa Höienloftssal* in the highvaulted hall; *i dyben Dal* in the deep valley.

174. The following adjectives do not add any *t* in the neuter:

1) Adjectives ending in a distinctly derivative s k: Ex.: *krigersk* warlike, *Norsk* Norwegian. But *rask* quick, *falsk* false, *frisk* and *fersk* fresh add *t*: *et raskt Löb* a quick run.

2) Adjectives ending in a vowel; except *aa: et sanddru Menneske* a truthful person; *et stille Vand* a quiet lake; *et öde Sted* a desolate place. But *et blaat Baand* a blue ribbon. Exceptions are further: *ny* new, *fri* free, N. *stö* steady; neut. *nyt, frit, stöt.*

3) Adjectives ending in *–t;* Ex.: *let* easy; and some adjectives ending in *–d: glad* joyful, *lad* lazy, *led* loathsome, *kaad* wanton, *ræd* frightened, *lærd* learned, *fremmed* strange and foreign words such as *absurd, nitid, solid, splendid.*

4) Furthermore those ending in –e s or –s with preceding consonant: *fælles* common, *afsides* out of the way; and *nymodens* newfangled, *stakkels* poor, *gjængs* current.

NOTE. With adjectives ending in –i g or –li g a *t* is added in neuter in writing, but neither *g* nor *t* is pronounced; see §§ (D.) 43 and (N.) 125.

175. A long vowel with or without a following *d* (Danish pron. ð, Norw. mute or pron. *t*) is shortened before the *t* of the neuter; Ex.: *blaat* of *blaa* blue, *bli(d)t* of *blid* (D. pr. blið, N. bli·) mild; *blö(d)t* of *blöd* (D. pr. bløð, N. bløt).

176. The following pronominal adjectives ending in –e n drop their *n* before the *t* of the neuter: *megen—meget* much, *mangen—mangt* many, *nogen* some, *ingen—intet* none; *anden—andet* other, *hvilken—hvilket* which, *en—et* one, *din—dit* your, *min—mit* my, *sin—sit* his, her; N. *liden—lidet*. So also past participles ending in –e n: *skreven—skrevet* written, *egen—eget* in the meaning of own; but in the meaning of peculiar *egent: et egent Menneske* a peculiar person; *særegen, særeget* and *særegent* peculiar, *voxen—voxent* adult, and in the same manner other adjectives which were originally past prtcpls. but are now used as pure adjectives: *et voxent Menneske* a grown-up person; but *han er voxet* he has grown.

NOTE. The adjective *liden* is now obsolete in Danish, only occasionally used in poetry, while it still continues to be the regular form in Norwegian. In Danish they use the originally definite form *lille* both as definite and indefinite, both as neuter and common gender. As plural of D. *lille* N. *liden* is employed *smaa*.

177. Adjectives ending in –e l, –e n and –e r drop the *e* of their last syllable before *e* of the plural or definite form: *gammel—gamle* old, *mager—magre* lean, *hoven—hovne* swollen.

Adjectives ending in an unstressed –e t form their plural and definite form in –e d e; Ex.: *stribet—stribede* stripet, but *let—lette* light, *violet—violette*.

NOTE. In Norwegian colloquial language the adjectives ending in –e t are often given the form of –e t e, even in the indefinite form; Ex.: *stripete* striped, *Veien er stenete* the road is stony.

178. The following adjectives do not add any –*e* in plural or in the definite form:

1) Those ending in –*e: stille* quiet, *ægte* genuine, *öde* desolate.

2) Those ending in –es or –s with preceding consonant. Exception: *tilfreds* satisfied always takes the –e, and *aflægs* obsolete, *dagligdags* commonplace, and *gammeldags* old-fashioned may take it; Ex.: *det altid tilfredse Barn* the always satisfied child.

3) Most adjectives ending in a stressed vowel; Ex.: *blaa* blue, *tro* faithful, *ædru* sober, *bly* bashful; *fri* and *ny* may in D. be written and pronounced with or without –e, *frie* and *nye* or *fri* and *ny*; in Norwegian always with –e: *nye*, *frie*; so also N. *stöe*.

179. The following adjectives lack the definite form in –e: *megen* much, *anden* other, *egen* own (but *egen* peculiar, *egne*). N. *liden* has the definite form *lille*.

These adjectives also have irregular plurals: *megen—mange*, *anden—andre*; *liden* uses as plural *smaa* small; *faa* few occurs only in plural; *smaa*, however, may also occur in singular, mostly neuter with collective words: *smaat Kvæg* small cattle, *den smaa* the little one.

NOTE. In Norwegian colloquial language *anden* may take the definite form *den andre* in stead of *den anden* the other.

180. Indeclinable are, besides those adjectives ending in –e, –es or –s with preceding consonant mentioned in §§ 174, 4 and 178, 1 and 2, the following: *idel* sheer, *lutter* mere, *nok* sufficient, *kvit* rid of, *alene* alone (only used predicatively), *var* in the expression *blive var* to become aware of (but N. adj. *var* cautious, is declinable). Also *lig* like, equal may in mathematics and elsewhere be used unchanged: *et Tal lig Summen af to andre* a number equal to the sum of two others.

181. Use of the definite form of the adjectives: The definite form of the adjective is used 1) after the definite article: *det store Hus* the big house; 2) after a possessive pronoun or a genitive; Ex.: *min nye Hat* my new hat; *min Kusines lyse Parasol* my cousin's light parasol; 3) after a demonstrative pronoun and after the relative pronoun *hvilken* which; Ex.: *dette höie Træ* this high tree, *hin sorte Kat* that black cat. *Han reddede med personlig Livsfare ti Menneskeliv, hvilken tapre Handling skaffede ham en Medalje* he saved with danger for his own life ten human lives, which brave deed procured him a medal; 4) in expressions of address and in apposition to a personal pronoun: *Kjære Ven* Dear friend, *jeg elendige Mand* I miserable man.

NOTE. For examples of the definite form of the adjective used with the postpositive article see § 153, Note 1.

182. Agreement of the adjective with its noun. The adjective must agree with its noun in gender and number both as **attribute, apposition** and **predicate.** *Et stort Hus* a big house, *store Huse* big houses; *Huset, et stort rödmalet* the house, a big red one, *Huset er stort* the house is big. *Vore Ansigter er(e) solbrændte* our faces are sunburnt. (As for the superlative forming an exception as predicate see § 189.)

II. COMPARISON OF ADJECTIVES.

183. The adjectives form their comparatives in –e re (–r e), superlative in –e s t (–s t).

   glad—glad   *gladere*   *gladest.*
   rig—rich   *rigere*   *rigest.*

Adjectives ending in –e add only –r e and –s t.

   ringe—slight   *ringere*   *ringest*

Adjectives ending in an unaccented −i g (−l i g) −s o m add in superlative only −s t :

fattig—poor *fattigere* *fattigst.*
nöisom—easily contented *nöisommere* *nöisomst.*

Adjectives ending in a single consonant with preceding short vowel double their final consonant before the comparative and superlative terminations :

smuk—nice *smukkere* *smukkest.*

Adjectives ending in an unstressed −e l, −e n, (see § 187, 1) −e r drop the −e before the comp. and superl. endings :

ædel—noble *ædlere* *ædlest.*
fager—fair *fagrere* *fagrest.*
fuldkommen—perfect *fuldkomnere* *fuldkomnest.*

184. The following adjectives form their comparative and superlative by adding −r e (−e r e) and −s t and at the same time modifying the radical vowel by mutation:

ung—young *yngre* *yngst.*
stor—great *större* *störst.*
tung—heavy *tyngre* *tyngst.*
or *tungere* *tungest.*
lang—long *længere* *længst.*

and irregularly:

faa—few *færre* *færrest.*

185. The following adjectives form their comparatives and superlatives of a different stem from the positive:

gammel—old *ældre* *ældst.*
god—good *bedre* *bedst.*
lille (liden)—little *mindre* *mindst.*
mange—many *flere* *flest.*
meget—much *mere* *mest.*
ond—bad *værre* *værst.*

ETYMOLOGY. 89

The adjective (and adv.) *nær* near forms its comparative and superlative by adding -m e r e, -m e s t : *nærmere nærmest*. In the same manner the adj. *fjern* far in Danish forms the comp. *fjærmer*, but only in the meaning of the off (horse).

186. The following comparatives and superlatives have no corresponding adjectives as positive (but there are corresponding adverbs):

(*nede*—down)   *nedre*—lower   *nederst*.
(*oven*—above)   *övre*—upper   *överst*.
(*ude*—without) *ydre*—outer   *yderst* (N. also pr. *ytterst*).
(*bag*—behind)   N. *bagre*—hind *bagerst*—hindmost.
(*inde*—within) *indre*—inner   *inderst*.
(*midt*—middle) *midtre*   *midterst*.
(*frem*—forward) *fremmere* (or *fremre*) *fremmest* (or *fremst*).

The following adjectives occur only in the comparative: *nordre* northern, *söndre* southern, *östre* eastern, *vestre* western.

In the superlative alone occur: *næst* next, *först* first, *forrest* foremost, *sidst* last, *ypperst* supreme, *mellemst* middle.

187. The following adjectives do not form any comparative and superlative. To denote the comparative and superlative meaning *mere* more and *mest* most are placed before the positive:

1) Most adjectives derived in -s k (-i s k) -e n and -e t : *mere krigersk* more warlike, *mest morderisk* most murderous. (But *friskere* fresher, *raskere* quicker, *hadskere* more rancorous, *glubskere* more ferocious, *harskere* more rancid.) *Vaagen*—awake, *mere vaagen*, *mest vaagen*. (But *modnere* more mature.) 2) Adjectives ending in -e s or -s with preceding consonant: *mere, mest afsides*, more, most out-of-the way; *mere, mest gjængs*, more, most current; also *mere fremmed* most strange. 3) Participles: *mere forslaaet* more beaten, *et*

mere vindende Væsen a more prepossessing manner. (But a few participles which have come to be used completely as adjectives may form comparative and superlative: *lærdere* more learned; *fuldkomnere* more perfect).

Some adjectives do not form any comparative and superlative on account of their signification; such are *evig* eternal, *udödelig* immortal etc.

INFLECTION AND USE OF THE COMPARATIVE AND SUPERLATIVE.

188. The comparative has only the form ending in –e: *den bedre Del* the better part; *et större Hus* a larger house. When used as a substantive it may take the genitive –s: *det gode er det bedres Fiende* the good [is the enemy of the better.

NOTE. Observe the use of the comparative to denote a pretty high degree. *En ældre Herre* an elderly gentleman; *et större Forretningshus* quite a large business house; *mindre* less is used as a less emphatic negative than *ikke* not, or a negative prefix. *Det var en mindre smuk Fremgangsmaade* that was not a very nice way of doing.

189. The superlative has as a rule the definite form when connected with a noun: *Den bedste Mand* the best man. *Det smukkeste Töi* the nicest cloth. But it occurs also in the indefinite form: *jeg har störst Lyst til ikke at gjöre det* I feel most inclined not to do it [but: *jeg har den största Lyst (af Verden) til ikke at gjöre det* I have the greatest mind not do it]. When used as a predicate the superlative as a rule is indeclinable, but may also take the definite article, and accordingly the definite form. *Dette Hus er störst* this house is largest. *Disse Bær er bedst* these berries are the best. But also: *dette Hus er det största* this house is the largest.

NOTE. The superlative may be emphasized by *aller* placed before the superlative: *allerbedst* best of all; *allerstörst* largest of all. This *aller* is an old gen. plur. (O. N. *allra* of *allr* all).

The Pronouns.

I. THE PERSONAL PRONOUNS.

190. The personal pronouns have a nominative and an oblique case, and some of them also have a possessive case. The personal pronoun for the 3d person has separate forms for masculine and feminine.

		1st person.	2d person.	3d person.	
				Masc.	Fem.
Sing.	Nom.	jeg	du	han	hun
	Poss.	—	—	hans	hendes
	Obl.	mig	dig	ham	hende
Plur.	Nom.	vi		de	
	Poss.	— (vores)	eders, (jers)	deres	
	Obl.	os	eder, jer	dem	

(*jeg* pron. Dan. jai, jæ, Nor. jei; *mig*, *dig* pron. Dan. mai, dai, mæ, dæ, Nor. mei, dei.)

NOTE 1. *jeg* and *du* have no corresponding possessive forms; in their stead are used the possessive pronouns (see § 192). Instead of poss. *vores* (which is mostly colloquial Danish) the poss. pron. *vor* is usually employed, while *eders* is more common than the corresponding poss. pron. *jer*. An antiquated form is *hannem* for *ham* him. *de* they is originally a demonstrative pronoun corresponding to the singular *den*, *det*. Analogously with *hannem* is formed *dennem* for *dem*.

NOTE 2. *Du* and *dig* thou, you is only used between members of the same family or near relatives (1st or 2d cousins) or between intimate friends (schoolmates or people acquainted since childhood, or those who have drunk "*dus*"), thus entering into a kind of fraternity that places them upon a footing of intimacy. The act of drinking *"dus'* is performed with certain ceremonies.

Note 3. Colloquially *han* and *hun* are often used referring to animals according to their natural gender, and in N. colloquially or rather vulgarly even to things according to the gender (masculine or feminine) which the noun in question has in colloquial Norwegian language.

II. THE REFLEXIVE AND RECIPROCAL PRONOUNS.

191a. The reflexive pronoun is *sig* (pronounce D. sai, N. sei), which can only be used in dependent functions, corresponding to a subject of 3d person, when the direct or indirect object is the same person or thing as the subject; Ex. *han slog sig* he hurt himself; N. *de satte sig paa Bænkene* they sat down upon the benches (but D. as a rule *de satte dem*, because in modern Danish *sig* is very rarely used referring to a subject of plural).

Sig is n e v e r used reflexively to *De* you: *slog De Dem?* did you hurt yourself?

Observe: *hver for sig* each for himself, separately.

191b. Reciprocal pronouns are *hinanden* and *hverandre*, one another each other. *Hinanden* should, according to the grammarians, be used referring to a subject consisting of two parties, *hverandre* to three or more. Ex.: *Han og hun saa hinanden for förste Gang* he and she saw each other for the first time. *Alle faldt om Halsen paa hverandre* they all threw themselves upon one another's necks.

But this rule of the grammarians is rarely observed in the spoken language.

III. THE POSSESSIVE PRONOUNS.

192. The possessive pronouns are :

	1st person sing.		2d person sing.		3d pers. refl. (sing. & pl.)	
	com.	neut.	com.	neut.	com.	neut.
Sing.	*min*	*mit*	*din*	*dit*	*sin*	*sit*
Plur.	*mine*		*dine*		*sine*	

	1st person plur.		2d person plur.	
Sing.	*vor*	*vort*	*jer*	*jert*
Plur.	*vore*		*jere*	

In stead of *jer, jert, jere* the gen. of the pers. pronoun *eders* is usually employed.

193. *sin, sit, sine* is only in Norway used referring to a subject of plur. In Denmark it is a rule to say: *Herrerne tog(e) deres Hatte* the gentlemen took their hats; in Norway they say: *Herrerne tog sine Hatte.*

Sin may refer to another word than the subject in such combinations as: *Giv hver sit* give each one his due.

When there besides the predicate verb is another verb (infinitive or participle) in the sentence *sin* may refer to the subject of either of these verbal forms, thus causing some ambiguity: *Hr. Pedersen bad Pigen hente sin Hat:* Mr. P. asked the servant girl to fetch his hat. But *Hr. Pedersen bad sin Ven tænde sin Cigar* Mr. P. asked his friend to light his (whose?) cigar. *Han fandt ham liggende i sin Seng* he found him lying in his bed (whose?). *Sin* may also refer to the logical subject of a noun indicating action: *hendes Kamp for sin Kongemagt* her fight for her royal power.

194. The possessive pronouns replace the missing genitive forms of the personal pronouns and are used in the same meanings and ways as the genitive of the nouns (see § 164). Observe the idiomatic expressions: *din Dumrian* you fool! *dit Fæ* you ass! etc.

The possessive pronouns cannot be combined with the pre-positive definite article. But in Norwegian they can colloquially be combined with nouns that have the postpositive definite article, in which case the pronoun is placed behind; Ex.: *Vennen min* my friend.

IV. DEMONSTRATIVE PRONOUNS.

195. Demonstrative pronouns are: *den* that, *denne* this, *hin* that, yonder.

		C. G.	N.	C. G.	N.	C. G.	N.
Sing.	Nom.	*den*	*det*	*denne*	*dette*	*hin*	*hint*
	Gen.	*dens*	*dets*	*dennes*	*dettes*	*hints*	*hints*
Plur.	Nom.	*de*		*disse*		*hine*	
	Gen.	*deres*		*disses*		*hines*	
	Obl.	*dem*					

When these pronouns are used adjectively, they are only subject to inflection as to numbers; Ex.: *Han valgte de Mænd* he chose those men; *disse Menneskers Öine er forblindede* the eyes of those people are blinded. *Hin* that, yonder is mostly a literary word; colloquially it is as a rule replaced by *den der* that there. *det* is often used where the English language requires the adv. so: *tror De det?* do you think so.

NOTE. *det* is used without stress like the English it as subj. of impersonal verbs, or as an "indicator" if the real subject is another sentence: *det regner* it rains; *det fortælles, at Kongen er död* it is said that the king is dead; *se efter, hvad det er, som staar paa* look what it is, that is the matter.

196. Among the demonstrative pronouns are as a rule, counted the pronominal adjectives *slig* such; *saadan* such; *begge* both; *samme* same; *selv* self. *Slig* has n. *sligt*, pl. *slige*, *saadan*, n. *saadant*, plur. *saadanne*. All these forms can take the gen. -s if the word is used substantively. *begge* and *samme* can take the genitive -s when used alone, but are otherwise indeclinable. *selv* is indeclinable, except that when used before a noun with the postpositive def. article it may add an -e: *selve Manden* the man himself. Observe that *selv* in Dano-Norwegian is used alone: *jeg skal gjöre det selv* I shal do it myself. The adv. *saa* may in some cases be used as a pronoun: *i saa Tilfælde* in such a case, *i saa Maade* in that respect, *i saa Henseende* in that respect.

V. INTERROGATIVE PRONOUNS.

197. Interrogative pronouns are: *hvo*, *hvem* which, *hvad* what, *hvilken* which. (The initial -h is mute in all these pronouns, see §§ D. 58, N. 126). *Hvo* and *hvem* refers to persons and are only used substantively. They have the genitive *hvis* whose; *hvo* is becoming obsolete and is chiefly used in poetry and elevated style. *Hvad* when used substantively only refers to things; when used as an adjective it may qualify names of living beings as well as of things and irrespective of gender. *Hvilken* is used adjectively and has the neuter *hvilket* pl. *hvilke*. When the interrogative pronouns are ruled by a preposition, the latter can be placed before the pronoun or at the end of the sentence. Ex. *Hvem er der* who is there? *Hvo ved, hvor nær mig er min Ende?* who knows how near my end might be? *Hvis Böger er det?* whose books is it? *Hvad siger De* what do you say? *Hvad Tjeneste kan jeg gjöre Dem* what service can I do you? *Hvilke Lande er(e) de rigeste?* what countries are the richest? *Hvilken Kjole har hun paa?* what dress does she wear? *Af hvem har De faaet Bogen?* from whom did you get the book? or *Hvem har De faaet Bogen af? Til hvem har han sagt det?* To whom has he told it? or *Hvem har han sagt det til?*

Hvad for en what, neut. *hvad for et*, plur. *hvad for* is used adjectively. *Hvad for en Mand er dette?* what man is this? *Hvad for et Hus er dette?* or *hvad er dette for et Hus?* what house is this? *Hvad for Kjör er dette?* what cows are these? (Obs. the use of the neuter *dette* in all these queries.) Note: *Hvilken* may be used in exclamations: *Hvilken Udsigt!* what a view! *Hvilken Skjönhed* what a beauty. The same meaning may in Danish be expressed by: *sikken*, contraction for *se hvilken* see what a; Ex. *sikken en nydelig Dame* what a beautiful lady, and in Norwegian by *for en: For en Sorg*, what a grief! *For en Dumrian du er!* what a fool you are!

VI. RELATIVE PRONOUNS.

198. Relative pronouns are: *som, der, hvilken, hvem. Som* and *der* are used substantively and are not inflected. As genitive is used *hvis* whose. *Hvilken* is used both adjectively and substantively and is inflected as the interrogative pronoun of the same form. *Som* is the general relative pronoun, which is used when there is no special reason to employ one of the others. It must always have the first place in the sentence and therefore when it should follow after a preposition this latter must be placed adverbially at the end of the sentence. *der* can only be used as subject and is chiefly employed when there is another *som* near by so as to avoid confusion and cacophony; Ex.: *den Mand som var her* the man who was here. *Det saa ud, som om den Mand, der var her, var syg* it looked as if the man who was here was sick. *Det Synspunkt, som han saa Sagen fra, var ikke det rigtige* the point of view from which he looked at the matter was not the right one.

hvem only refers to persons and can never be used as subject; Ex.: *en Gjæst hvem fyrstelig Æresbevisning tilkommer* a guest to whom princely honor is due.

hvilken refers to persons and things. The neuter *hvilket* sometimes refers not to any single word in the preceding sentence, but to the whole sentence; Ex.: *der blev en skarp Frost med haardt Veir, hvilket Hedningerne tilskrev Gudernes Vrede* a piercing cold set in with rough weather, something that the heathen attributed to the wrath of the gods. With the same meaning may be used *hvad* what, a pronoun that otherwise only refers to the word *alt* all, everything; Ex.: *alt, hvad jeg har, er dit* everything I have is yours.

NOTE. The relative pronoun may be omitted except as subject; Ex.: *den eneste Ko, han eiede, blev funden död* the only cow he owned was found dead. In antiquated language and sometimes in poetry the relative may be omitted also as subject, but then the verb must be preceded by another word; Ex.: *alle smaa Fugle, i Skoven var* all the little birds that were in the wood; *den Mand, her staar* the man, who stands here.

199. *hvo, hvem, hvad*, may sometimes perform functions at the same time in the principal and in the subordinate proposition. They are then called **indefinite relative pronouns**. After these pronouns may sometimes be added *som* or *der*, in which case these indefinite relative pronouns to a certain extent act as demonstratives. *Hvo som staar, se til, at han ikke falder* whoever stands, see that he does not fall. *Hvem der gjör det, skal miste sit Liv* whoever does that, shall lose his life. *Hvad du har gjort, er tilstrækkeligt* what you have done, is sufficient. The indefinite meaning is emphasized in: *hvemsomhelst som* whoever, *hvadsomhelst som* whatever, *hvilkensomhelst som* whichever.

VII. INDEFINITE PRONOUNS.

200. Indefinite pronouns are: *man, en, hver, enhver, enhversomhelst, hvilkensomhelst, hvemsomhelst, hvadsomhelst.*

man corresponds to the French o n, German m a n. English has no exact equivalent. It can only be used as subject; Ex.: *man siger* they say, it is said.

en is originally the numeral one; it has the same meaning as *man*, but is not in its use limited to being subject of the sentence; Ex.: *det gjör en ondt at se saadanne Kræfter gaa tilspilde* it pains a man to see such abilities wasted.

hver or *enhver* each, every; gen. *hvers, enhvers;* neut. *hvert, ethvert; alle og enhver* each and everyone; *hver eneste* every single one; *enhversomhelst, hvemsomhelst* everybody; *hvilkensomhelst,* neut. *hvilketsomhelst,* plur. *hvilkesomhelst* which(so)ever, any; *hvadsomhelst* what(so)ever, anything. These pronouns together with the relative *som* form indefinite relative pronouns (see § 199).

201. Among the indefinite pronouns are as a rule counted the indefinite numerals: *nogen* some one, *mangen* many a, *ingen* none, *alle* all, *somme* some, *anden* other.

nogen some one, neut. *noget,* gen. *nogens, nogets,* plur. *nogle,* gen. *nogles. nogen* also means any; then it has plur. *nogen* (like singular). *Har De n o g e n Penge?* Have you any money? *Ja, jeg har n o g l e Kroner.* Yes, I have a few crowns. Instead of *noget* used substantively may be said *nogenting* something, anything.

NOTE. Colloquially the plur. is always *nogen*, in eastern Norway pron. *non, nɔɔn*.

mangen many a, neut. *mangt;* usually occurring in plur *mange* many, gen. *mangens, mangts, manges*. *Jeg har mange Penge* I have much money. *Mangen en* many a, neut. *mangt et*. *ingen* none, neut. *intet*, plur. *ingen*, gen. *ingens, intets*. *Ingen* may be connected with a noun in plur. or in singular; plural is used whenever in affirmative case a plural would have been expected; Ex.: *der var ingen Mennesker der* there were no people there; *intet Menneske har set ham* nobody has seen him. Emphasized *ingensomhelst* none whatever. Instead of *intet* used substantively may be said *ingenting* nothing.

anden other, neut. *andet*, plur. *andre*, gen. *andres* etc. *nogle—andre* some—others, *en—en anden* one—another.

al all, neut. *alt*, plur. *alle*, gen. *alts, alles;* the common gender sing. can not be used as a substantive and accordingly cannot take the gen. *s;* subst. *alting* everything, *altsammen, allesammen* all and every one.

somme some is a somewhat antiquated word; *somme Kjærringer ere slige* some women are that way.

THE NUMERALS.

202. The following is a list of the numerals:

A. Cardinals.   B. Ordinals.

  1 *en (een)*, neut. *et (ét,* D. *eet,* N. *ett)* *förste*
  2 *to* *andet*
  3 *tre* *tredie*

A. Cardinals.	B. Ordinals.
4 *fire*	*fjerde*
5 *fem*	*femte*
6 *seks (sex)*	*sjette*
7 *syv*	*syvende*
8 *otte*	*ottende*
9 *ni*	*niende*
10 *ti*	*tiende*
11 *elleve*	*ellevte*
12 *tolv*	*tolvte*
13 *tretten*	*trettende*
14 *fjorten*	*fjortende*
15 *femten*	*femtende*
16 N. *seksten (sexten)*, D. *sejsten*	*sextende*
17 *sytten*	*syttende*
18 *atten*	*attende*
19 *nitten*	*nittende*
20 *tyve*	*tyvende*
21 *en og tyve*	*enogtyvende*
22 *to og tyve*	*toogtyvende*
30 *tredive*, N. also *tretti*	*tredivte*, N. also *trettiende*
35 *fem og tredive*	*femogtredivte*
40 D. *fyrretyve, fyrre*, N. *firti, førti, før*	D. *fyrretyvende*, N. *firtiende, førtiende*
50 D. *halvtredsindstyve, halvtreds*, N. *femti*	D. *halvtredsindstyvende*, N. *femtiende*
60 D. *tresindstyve, tres*, N. *seksti*	D. *tresindstyvende*, N. *sekstiende*
70 D. *halvfjerdsindstyve, halvfjerds*, N. *sytti*	D. *halvfjerdsindstyvende*, N. *syttiende*
80 D. *firsindstyve, firs*, N. *otti, otteti*	D. *firsindstyvende*, N. *ottiende*

A. Cardinals.	B. Ordinals.
90 D. *halvfemsindstyve,* *halvfems,* N. *niti, nitti*	D. *halvfemsindstyvende,* N. *nittiende*
100 *hundrede*	
101 *hundrede og en,* neut. *Hundrede og et*	*hundrede og förste*
129 *hundrede og ni og tyve*	*hundrede og ni og tyvende*
1000 *tusind(e),* N. *tusend(e)*	

The cardinals are all uninflected save *en,* neut. *et,* which, to distinguish it from the indefinite article, is often written (D.) *een,* (N.) *én;* neut. (D.) *eet,* (N.) *ét, ett.* But with the definite article always *den ene.*

203. The ordinals are used only in the weak or definite form, excepting *anden* second; *den anden* the second or the other (N. colloquially *den andre*), plur. *andre* others.

hundred(e) and *tusind(e)* have no corresponding ordinals. In arithmetics the cardinals are also used as ordinals, but otherwise the use of the ordinals of these words is avoided as much as possible. *En Hundrededel* one hundredth part; *en Tusindedel* one thousandth part. (D.) *Jeg siger dig det for ni og halvfemsindstyvende Gang;* (N.) *Jeg siger dig det for ni og nittiende Gang* I tell you so for the hundredth time.

204. The cardinals *halvtredsindstyve* 50 etc. are exclusively used in Denmark and by the older generation in southern Norway. *Femti, seksti* etc. are used in most parts of Norway by all ages and classes of the people and by the younger generation all over the country. The abbreviated form *halvtreds* etc. are only used when the numerals occur alone, the full forms are used in connection with a noun. *For halvtredsindstyve Aar siden* fifty years ago. *I Aaret femti* in the year fifty.

NOTE. The forms *tresindstyve* etc. are to be explained in the following manner: *tre–sinds–tyve*=three times twenty. *sinds* is a form of an old noun occurring in *denne sinde* this time, *nogensinde* anytime etc. For explanation of the forms *halvtred–sindstyve* etc. see § 205.

205. One and a half is called *halvanden*, 2½ *halvtredje*, 3½ *halvfjerde* etc. (hence *halvtredsindstyve* etc. see § 204).

At 3 o'cl. is: *Klokken tre;* half past two: *Klokken halv tre; halv fire, halv fem* etc. Ten minutes past five: *ti Minuter over fem;* ten minutes off three: *ti Minuter i tre* (or *til tre);* fifteen minutes past six: *et Kvartér over seks;* it is twenty minutes past five: *Klokken mangler ti Minuter paa* (or *i*) *halvseks;* at 7.40: *ti Minuter over halv otte;* at 9.45: *tre Kvartér til ti.* It is 9.45: *Klokken mangler et Kvartér paa ti.*

selvanden, selvtredje etc. with one, two etc. others; *jeg var her igaar selvtredje* I was here yesterday with two others.

en Trediedel one third; *en Fjerdedel* one fourth etc.; *ni Tyvendedele* nine twentieth parts.

Obs. *en Procent* one percent. *pro anno* per annum.

For det förste in the first place, *for det andet* in the second place, *for det tredje* etc. in the third place etc.

NOTE. *et Snes* a score (the unity always used by the sale of eggs) *en Tylvt* a dozen (boards etc.) *et Dusin* a dozen (buttons etc.) *et Gros* 12 dozen

---

THE VERBS.

206. The verbs in the Danish and Dano-Norwegian language have separate forms for voices, tenses and to a certain extent modes and numbers.

The forms of the verbs are either simple or compound (formed by means of an auxiliary verb).

The verbs are divided into two classes—the **weak** (also called regular) and the **strong** (or irregular) according to the formation of the imperfect and past participle.

207. The **present** tense of all verbs is formed alike, namely by adding –e r (in a few cases –r) to the theme of the verb (or –r to the infinitive form); Ex.: *jeg elsk–er* I love; *han bring–er* he brings; *du læs–er* you read; *han tru–er* he threatens. Present **plural** is in written language, when used, formed by dropping the final –r of the singular.

The **infinitive** is formed by adding -e to the theme of the verb: *elsk–e, bring–e, tru–e.*

Some verbs the root of which ends in a stressed vowel form their present by adding only –r and use their root unchanged as infinitive; Ex.: *staa* stand, pres. *staar*; *gaa* go, pres. *gaar*; *at bo* to reside; *at dö* to die; *at sy* to sew; *at se* to see.

Some verbs have double forms in infinitive, with or without –e: *du* or *due* to be fit; *di* or *die* to suck; *fri* or *frie*, *befri* or *befrie* to liberate; *vi* or *vie* to wed, to consecrate; *forny* or *fornye* to renew; all these verbs in Danish form their present in –e r: *duer, dier* etc.

NOTE: In Norwegian the infinitive of these verbs is with the exception of *fri* and *befri* formed in –e.

–e is written and pronounced in the following verbs: *bie* to wait; *tie* to be silent; *grue* to dread; *kue* to cow; *true* to threaten; *skrue* to screw; *lue* to blaze; *bejae* to answer in the affirmative.

The **present participle** of all verbs is formed by adding *–ende* to the theme of the verb: *löb–ende* running, *gaaende* walking.

The **passive** or **medial voic** is formed in –e s and in a few cases in –s.

A. WEAK VERBS.

208. The weak verbs are divided into three classes; those belonging to the **first class** form their **imperfect** in –ede, their **past participle** in –et.

I. PARADIGM OF VERBS OF THE 1ST CLASS.

elske to love.

A. Active.
  1) Simple forms.

	Ind.	Subj.	Imp.	Inf.	Partcpl.
Pres.: Sing.	*elsk-er,*	*elsk-e*	*elsk,*	*at elsk-e*	*elsk-ende*
Plur.	*elsk-e*		*elsk-er*		

Imperf. (*jeg* etc., *vi* etc.)
  elske-de

  2) Forms compound with past participle:

Perfect.: Sing *har elsket*   *at have elsket*
    Plur. *have elsket*
Pluperf.: (sing. and plur.) *havde elsket*

  3) Forms compound with pres. infinitive:

Future: Sing. *skal* or *vil elske*   *at skulle* or *ville elske*
    Plur. *skulle* or *ville elske*
Conditional (sing. and plur.) *skulde* or *vilde elske*

  4. Doubly compound forms:

Compound future:
  Sing. *skal* or *vil have elsket*   *at skulle* or *ville have elsket*
  Plur. *skulle* or *ville have elsket*

B. Passive.
  1) Simple forms:

	Ind.	Infinitive.	
Present:	*elskes*	*at elskes*	
Imperf.:	*elskedes*		Past Partcpl.: *elsket*

2) Compound forms:

	Ind.	Inf.
Pres.: Sing.	*bliver elsket*	*at blive elsket*
Plur.	*blive elskede*	

3) Doubly compound forms:

Perfect: Sing. *er bleven elsket*   *at være bleven elsket*
        or *har været elsket*   or *at have været elsket*
    Plur. *ere blevne elskede* or *have været elskede*

Pluperf.: Sing. *var bleven elsket* or *havde været elsket*
    Plur. *vare blevne elskede* or *havde været elskede*

Fut.: Sing. *skal* or *vil blive elsket*   *at skulle* or *ville blive elsket* or *at skulle elskes*
       or *skal elskes*
    Plur. *skulle* or *ville blive elskede* or *skulle elskes*

Conditional: *skulde* or *vilde blive elsket* or *skulde elskes*

209. In this manner are inflected almost all d e r i v a t i v e verbs ending in a vowel or in a combination of consonants with which the ending –t e does not readily agree.

In poetry verbs ending in a vowel often drop –e before the ending –d e, and an apostrophe is written in its place, *befri'de*. In N o r w a y verbs ending in a vowel colloquially form their imperf. in –d d e and this form is now often used also in literature.   *naadde* reached; *trodde* believed; etc. in stead of *naaede, troede*.

In forms such as *elskede* the final -e is often dropped colloquially and in poetry: *elsked'* for *elskede*. In N o r w a y it takes the form *elsket*, a form that also is commencing to appear in the literature.

Verbs ending in –l e and –r e with a preceding consonant have their imperative of the same form as their infinitive: *handle!* act; *logre*, wag your tail! But imperative of such words is in writing as much as possible avoided and colloquially *handl! logr!* are the common forms. Verbs in –n e with preceding consonant form their imperative regularly: *vaagn op*, wake up; *syyn hen!* languish.

210. Verbs belonging to the s e c o n d c l a s s form their i m p e r f e c t by adding –te, p a s t p a r t i c i p l e by adding –t without change of the radical vowel.

Inf. *at rose* to praise, pres. *roser*, impf. *roste*, past partc. *rost*.

(The other forms can easily be formed by comparison with the paradigm given of the first class).

In this manner are conjugated a great number of verbs ending in a single consonant (–b, –d, –g, –l, –r, –n, –s) with a preceding long vowel, or in the double consonant –m m or the combinations –l d and –n g; Ex.: *raabe* to cry, *raabte* (but *haabe* to hope, *haabede*); *koge* to cook, *kogte* (but *toge* to march in procession, *togede*); *tömme* to empty, *tömte* (but *svömme* swim, *svömmede* coll. *svömte*.

Obs. *have* to have, pres. *har*, pl. *have*, impf. *havde; dö* to die, impf. *döde*, ptcp. *död; ske* happen, imp. *skete* or *skede*, ptcp. *skeet*.

211. Verbs of the t h i r d c l a s s add in impf. –te (–d e), partcp. –t and at the same time change the radical vowel from –æ or –ø in infinitive to resp. –a and –u (–o) in impf.

NOTE: This change of vowel is explained by the fact that the infinitive of these verbs which in the old language ended in –j a, has the form with mutation, while in imperf. there was no reason for mutation, so the original radical vowel again appeared there (retro-mutation, G. Rückumlaut, D. *Gjenomlyd*).

To this class belong:

kvæle to stifle,	*kvalte*	*kvalt*.
lægge to lay,	*lagde*	*lagt*.

sætte to set,	*satte*	*sat,*
tælle to count,	*talte*	*talt.*
række*) to stretch,	*rakte*	*rakt.*
strække**) to stretch,	*strakte*	*strakt.*
tække to roof,	*takte*	*takt.*
vække to arouse,	*vakte*	*vakt.*
vænne to accustom,	*vante*	*vant.*
træde to tread, to step	*traadte*	*traadt.*
dölge conceal	*dulgte*	*dulgt.*
fölge follow	*fulgte*	*fulgt.*
spörge ask	*spurgte*	*spurgt.*
smöre smear	*smurte*	*smurt.*

Irregular:

sælge sell	*solgte*	*solgt.*
sige say	*sagde*	*sagt*
bringe bring	*bragte*	*bragt.*

NOTE 1: *vænne, tække, strække, vække* as a rule follow the first class: *vænnede, vænnet* etc.; this is in N. always the case with *tække*.

NOTE 2: *bringe* is an originally German word and has retained its German inflexion. The Old Norse form of *sige* was *segja* which explains the modern imperf. *sagde*. Of *eie* to own sometimes in poetry occurs the antiqu. imperf. *aatte*

NOTE 3: Present of *gjöre* is *gjör* and of *spörge* colloquially and in antiquated style *spör*, a form that is commencing to be introduced again into Norw. literature.

B. STRONG VERBS.

212. The strong verbs form their imperfect by changing the vowel (gradation, ablaut, *Aflyd*) without any termi-

---

*) But N. *række* to reach is strong: *rak, rukket*.
**) But N. *strække til* to be sufficient: *strak, strukket*.

nal addition. Past. ptcp. in these verbs regularly has the ending –e n for common gender and –e t for neuter, but of many verbs only the latter form can be used, and others while forming a strong imperf. form their prtcp. according to the weak conjugation. The vowel of the participle is sometimes that of the present, sometimes that of the imperf.

The strong verbs are divided into 6 classes depending upon the vowels occurring in the different forms (gradation series):

1.	*i* (*œ, e*)	*a*	*u*
2.	*i* (*e*)	*a*	*i* (*e*) or *aa*
3.	*i*	*e*	*e* (*i*)
4.	*y*	*ö*	*u* (*ö, y*)
5.	*a*	*o*	*a*
6.	No apparent gradation, in historical grammars called the reduplicating class.		

213. Class I.

i (*œ, e*)—*a*—*u*. Ex.: *binde* to bind, *bandt, bunden; sprække* to crack, *sprak, sprukken; finde* to find; *rinde* to run (of running water); *spinde* to spin; *stinke* to stink (ptcp. *stinket); svinde* to vanish; *tvinde* to twist; *vinde* to win; *klinge* to sound (ptcp. *klinget); springe* to spring; *svinge* to swing; *tvinge* to force; *synge* to sing (*sang, sungen,* poet. and ant. *sjunge); synke* to sink (*sank, sunket); slippe* to let go; *briste* to burst (inf.); *drikke* to drink (*drak, drukket; drukken* adj. drunk); *stikke* to stab (poet. and ant. *stinge, stak, stungen); brække* to break; N. *række* to reach; N. *strække til* to suffice; *trække* to draw; *fornemme* to perceive (ptcpl. *fornemmet* or *fornummet*); *hjælpe* to help; N. *brænde* to burn, (intr. *brandt,* ptcp. *brændt;* D. impf. *brændte); hænge* to hang, *hang* or *hængte, hængt;* N. *slænge* to loiter (*slang, slængt;* but

---

*) N. *rende, rendte, rendt* to run.

D. N. *slænge* to fling, *slængte*); *gjælde**) to be worth, to refer to (*gjaldt, gjældt*); N. *smælde* to make a noise (*smaldt* or *smældede, smældte,* ptc. *smældt*); *skjælve* to shiver, (*skjalv* or *skjælvede,* N. *skalv, skjælvet*); *knække* to crack, *knækkede* or *knak, knækket; sprætte* to sprawl, imperf. N. *sprat,* D. *sprættede, sprættet; skvætte* to get a start, N. *skvat, skvættede, skvættet.*

NOTE 1. When there is a double set of forms in imperf., a strong one and a weak one, the strong form has originally represented the intransitive meaning, the weak form the transitive; Ex.: *han strakte sin Haand ud* he stretched his hand forth; *Pengene strak ikke til* the money was not sufficient; *Huset brandt op* the house burned down; *jeg brændte mine Skibe* I burned my ships; *jeg skvat tilside* I jumped aside; *Pigen skvættede Vand paa mig* the girl splashed water on me; *jeg hængte min Hat paa Knagen* I hung my hat on the rack; *Manden hang i Galgen* the man was hanging in the gallows.

NOTE 2. Antiquated and poet. Danish are the imperf. plurals: *funde, runde, svunde, sprunge, stunge, sunge, drukke, hjulpe.*

214. Class II.

i (*e*)—*a*—*i* (*e*) or *aa*. Ex.: *give* to give, *gav, givet; bede* to pray, *bad, bedt* (*bedet*). To this class belong: *give* to give; *gide* to prevail upon one's self to, *gad, gidet; sidde* to sit, *sad, siddet; kvæde* to sing, *kvad, kvædet; være* to be, *var, været; bære* to wear, *bar, baaren; skjære* to cut, *skar, skaaren; stjæle* to steal, *stjal, stjaalen; se* to se, *saa, seet; ligge* to lie, *laa, ligget; æde* to eat, *aad, ædt.*

NOTE 1. *dræbe* to kill, although regularly following the weak conjugation (*dræbte, dræbt*) occurs in N. poetry in the strang impf. *drap: han drap far* he killed my father (Björnson).

NOTE 2. To the infinitive *være*, to be, corresponds the pres. (jeg) er I am (pl. *ere*), but *overvære*, to be present at, has pres. *overværer*, imp. *overvar,*, and *undvære* to be without, *undværer, undværede.*

---

*) always weak: *undgjælde* to pay the penalty of, *gjengjælde* to requite.

NOTE 3. Some of these verbs may in Danish form their impf. plural in -e: *bare, aade* etc.

215. Class III.

i—e—e (*i*). Ex.: *gribe* to catch, *greb, greben; bide* to bite, *bed, bidt; hvine* to shriek, *hven* or *hvinede, hvinte, hvinet); grine* to grin (N. *gren*, D. *grinede* or *grinte, grinet); trine* to step (*tren, trinet); gribe* to catch; *knibe* to pinch; *pibe* to pipe (*peb, pebet*); *slibe* to grind (*sleb, slebet*, N. pron. *slipt; sleben* adj. polished); *blive* to become (*blev, bleven*); *drive* to drive; *hive* to heave (impf. D. *hivede*, N. *hev, hevet); rive* to tear; *skrive* to write (all these as *blive*); *bide; glide* to slide (*gled, gleden*, N. pron. *glidd); lide* to wear on (*led, leden*); *lide* to suffer (*led, lidt); ride* to ride (*red, redet*, N. pron. *ridd*); *skride* to proceed (*skred, skredet); slide* to wear (*sled, slidt*); *smide* to fling (*smed, smidt*); *stride* to fight (*stred, stridt*); *svide* to singe (*sved, sveden*, N. pron. *svidd); vride* to wringe (*vred, vreden*, N. pron. *vridd*); *kige* (pron. Nor. *kjikke*) to peep (*keg* or *kigede, keget* or *kiget); snige* to sneak (*sneg, sneget*); *svige* to deceive (*sveg, svegen*); *vige* to yield (*veg, veget*).

NOTE. These verbs may in Danish form their ipf. pl. in -e: *bleve, vege* etc. (but not *bede*, because that would be liable to be confounded with *bede* plur. pres. of *at bede* to pray).

216. Class IV.

y—ö—u (*ö, y*). Ex.: *krybe* to crawl, *kröb, kröben; bryde* to break, *bröd, brudt; fyge* to drift (prtc. *föget*); *ryge**) to smoke (*det ryger* it smokes), *rög, röget; stryge* to stroke (ptcp. *strögen); klyve* to climb (N. imperf. *klöv*, D. *klyvede*, ptc. N. *klövet*, D. *klyvet*); N. *skyve* to push (*skjöv, skjövet*); *flyve* to fly (*flöi, flöiet*); *lyve* to lie (*löi, löiet*); *byde* to bid

---

*) Usually intr.; in transitive meaning is in Norway used *röge: at röge Tobak* to smoke tobacco (impf. *rögte*, ptcp. *rögt*).

(ptc. *buden, budt*); *bryde* *) to break; *flyde* to flow (ptc. *flydt*); *gyde* to pour (*gjöd* or D. *göd, gydt*); *lyde* to obey (ptc. *lydt*); *nyde* to enjoy (*nydt*); *skryde* to boast (*skrydt*); *snyde* to cheat)—ptc. *snydt;* *skyde* to shoot (*skjöd*, ptc. *skudi*); *fortryde* to regret (ptc. *fortrudt*); *betyde* to signify (D. *betöd* or *belydede*, N. *betydde***) or *betöd*, ptc. *betydet*); *syde* to boil (generally *sydede*, prt. *sydet*); *fnyse* to fret (*fnös* or *fnyste*, ptc. *fnyset, fnyst*); *fryse* to be cold (*frös—frosset*); *gyse* to shudder (*gjös, gös, gyste—gyst*); *nyse* to sneeze (ptc. *nyst*).

NOTE. The imperfect *frös, fnös, nös, gjös* do not regularly form any plural in —*e* in Danish. *töd* is in Danish an antiquated imperf. of *tude* to howl, while in Norway *töt* is impf. of *tyte* to ooze out.

217. Class V.

a— o— a.

befale to command (*befalede* or ant. *befol, befalet*); *gale* to crow (*galede* or *gol, galet*); *fare* to travel (*for, faret*); *lade* to let (*lod, ladet*); *grave* to dig (*gravede* or *grov, gravet*); *drage* to draw (*drog, dragen*); *jage* to hunt (*jagede* or *jog, jagen*); *tage* to take (*tog, tagen*).

Irregular are:

slaa to strike (*slog, slaaet* or *slagen*); *staa* to stand (*stod, staaet*); *sværge* to swear (*svor, svoren*); *le* to laugh (*lo, leet*);

NOTE: *befalede* is now exclusively used in common speech; so is *galede;* *jagede* is more common than its corresponding strong form. *jage* is always weak when it indicates to go hunting. *Han blev slagen* he was conquered: *han blev slaaet* he was struck.

---

* Not to be confounded with *bryde* to trouble, in Danish regularly conjugated: impf. *bröd*—ptc. *brydt* (or *brudt*), N. *brydde* (or *bröd*), ptc. *brydd*. That these two words are originally different is seen from the fact that *bryde* to trouble in Norway is pronounced *bry*, while *bryde* to break is pronounced *bryte*.

**) Always *betydede* when signifying: gave to understand.

An antiquated inf. and present for *staa* and *staar* is *stande, stander;* imperative *stat*, plur. *stander*, partc. *standet*.

Antiquated is *vov* for *vævede* of *væve* to weave; also *vog* imfpf. of *veie* in the meaning: to kill; in the meaning: to weigh, in which it is now exclusively used in common speech *veie* has impf. *veiede*.

218. Class VI.

Apparently no gradation in the different tenses. The following verbs belong to this class:

löbe to run,	*löb*	*löbet*.
sove to sleep,	*sov*	*sovet*.
græde*) to weep,	*græd*	*grædt*.

D. *hedde* (N. *hede*) to be called, *hed* (D. also *hedte*), *hedt*. *hugge* to cut, N. *hug* (D. commonly *huggede*), *hugget*.

komme to come,	*kom*	*kommen*.	
falde to fall,	*faldt*	*falden*,**)	*faldt*.
holde to hold,	*holdt*	*holdt*.†)	

To this class are also counted:

faa to get,	*fik*	*faaet* (N. pron. *fåt*.)
gaa to go,	*gik*	*gaaet* (N. pron. *gåt*.)

Wholly irregular is: *tie* to be silent, *taug* (N. *tiede*, pron. *tidde*,) ptcp. *tiet*.

NOTE: None of these verbs form an impf. plural in –e.

219.

When there are two sets of verbs, one strong and one weak, the former originally was intransitive the latter transitive. But this difference, to a great extent, has been wiped out, both forms now being largely used promiscuously;

---

*)N. also *graate*. **)*falden* usually refers to a moral downfall; *falden fra Himlen* (*himmelfalden*) fallen from the skies, struck with amazement. †)*holden* is an adj. well-to-do.

see remarks to *hængte* and *hang*, *brændte* and *brandt* (213 Note 1) It is very common in Norway to say: *jeg har lagt i min Seng* I have laid in my bed, (ptcp. of *lægge* to lay) instead of: *jeg har ligget i min Seng* I have been lying in my bed, (ptcp. of *ligge* to lie); in the same manner: *jeg har nu sat her en Time* I have now set here an hour (ptc. of *sætte* to set) instead of: *jeg har nu siddet her en Time* I have now been sitting here for an hour. But in the following pairs of verbs the distinction is complete: *springe—sprænge* to spring and to burst, *falde—fælde* to fall and to fell; *synke, sænke* to sink (intr. and trans.)

IRREGULAR VERS.

220. The following verbs have an irregular inflection.

Pres.		Imperf.	Partcp.	Inf.
Sing.	Plur.			
kan can	*kunne*	*kunde*	*kunnet*	*at kunne*
skal shall	*skulle*	*skulde*	*skullet*	*at skulle*
bör ought to	*bör*	*burde*	*burdet*	*at burde*
tör dare	*tör*	*turde*	*turdet*	*at turde*
maa must	*maa* (subj. *maatte*)	*maatte*	*maattet*	*at maatte*
vil will	*ville*	*vilde*	*villet*	*at ville*
ved know	*vide*	*vidste*	*vidst*	*at vide*

These verbs are in historical grammars generally called preteritopresents, because the forms now used as their present tenses are original imperfects. Hence the change of vowel between pres. sing. and plural (*ved—vide, skal—skulle*).

To this class also belongs the antiquated imperf. *aatte* ptc. *aatt* owned corresponding to the present inf. *eie*, regular impf. and ptc. *eiede, eiet;* also *mon* and *monne* used in antiquated style promiscuously as pres. or imperf. periphrastically with infinitives like English d o t h and d i d.

THE USE OF THE NUMBERS.

221. In colloquial language there is no distinction between singular and plural, the singular form being used with plural as well as with singular subjects. In written language the plural form in the present tense is still retained by most Danish authors and according to official Danish rules of spelling, while most Norwegian authors and the official Norwegian rules of spelling have dropped the distinction between singular and plural. In the imperf. of the weak verbs there can be no distinction. In the imperf. of the strong verbs the rule is about the same as in the present, although the plural form of some verbs is avoided even by Danish authors as stated in §§ 216 note, 218 note. As a general rule it can be said that the imperf. plural is not formed whenever it would have the same form as the present plural. In poetry plural or singular forms are used promiscuously with a subject in the plural according to the necessities of prosody. Ex.: *Kvinder selv stod op og strede* (Bjørnson) even women arose and fought (arose to fight).

THE USE OF THE TENSES.

222. The present tense is often employed with future meaning, Ex.: *jeg reiser imorgen* I shall depart to-morrow;

naar jeg ser ham, skal jeg hilse ham fra dig when I see him I shall bring him your greeting.

The present tense may also be employed to signify the past. *Igaar medens jeg gaar paa Gaden ser jeg pludselig en Mand komme löbende imod mig* yesterday while walking in the street I suddenly see a man coming running towards me.

223. The **imperfect** is used in conditional sentences referring to the present as in English; Ex. *hvis jeg vidste hans Navn, saa vilde jeg fortælle dig det* if I knew his name I should tell it to you. In the same manner the **pluperfect** is used in conditional sentences referring to the past: *om jeg havde set ham, skulde jeg nok ikke have ladet ham löbe* if I had seen him I should certainly not have let him skip.

224. In the future tense *skal* and *vil* as a rule have retained some of their original signification of duty and necessity or will and desire and they are used accordingly. There is no distinction as to the use in the different persons as in English. *Skal* is used in promises: *jeg skal sikkert have Klæderne færdig i rette Tid* I shall surely have the suit ready in time. For the use of *skal* and *vil* in the passive voice see §233.

The compound future more commonly takes the form of *faar elsket* (*faar* with past ptc.) instead of *skal have elsket*. Ex. *naar jeg faar gjort det, skal jeg lade Dem det vide* when I shall have done it (or when I get it done) I shall give you word.

In Norwegian *faa* with infinitive is used to express necessity: *jeg faar nok gjöre det, enten jeg vil eller ikke* I guess I shall have to do it whether I want to or not, (cfr. Engl. I've got to do it.)

225. Some intransitive verbs indicating a change form their perfect by means of *være* instead of *have*, when it is intended to express only that something has taken place without emphasizing the notion of action. *Han er gaaet* he is gone. *Min Fader er reist for en Time siden* my father left (has left) an hour ago; *Blomsten var visnet, för jeg fik den* the flower had faded before I got it. But: *jeg har gaaet fem Mil idag* I have walked five miles to-day. *Min Ven har reist fem Gange over Atlanterhavet* my friend has crossed the Atlantic five times.

THE USE OF THE MODES.

226. The subjunctive which only occurs in the present tense and has the same form as the infinitive is used in an optative or concessive meaning: *Leve Fædrelandet!* Long live our native land! *det koste hvad det vil* i. e. at all hazards.

227. The infinitive is as a rule used together with the particle *at* to. *Jeg önsker at tale med Dem* I wish to speak to you. The infinitive is used without *at* after the so called modal auxiliaries *burde, gide, kunne, maatte, monne, skulle, turde, ville;* Ex. *jeg tör paastaa, at han er en stor Slyngel* I dare assert that he is a great scoundrel. *Du bör gjöre det* you ought to do it. If *bör* (in antiquated style) is used impersonally in the meaning of "behoves to," then the following infinitive takes *at*: *eder bör at give efter* it behoves you to yield. The infinitive is also after some verbs used without *at* when it is a predicate to the object of the sentence, the same as in English: *jeg kan höre Hjertet banke* I can hear the heart beat. *Han lod de andre faa et langt Forspring* (N. *Forsprang*)he allowed the others to get a good lead. After other verbs the infinitive with *at* is used: *jeg fandt ham at være en brav Mand* I found him to be an honest man (more common:

jeg fandt, at han var etc.) *Jeg bad ham komme, at komme* or *om at komme* I asked him to come.

After *lade* to let, in the meaning of "to have" with a participle, "to cause to be done," the Dano-Norwegian language uses infinitive with an object of its own, placed before the infinitive: *jeg lod Huset bygge* I had the house built; *Generalen lod Forræderen skyde* the general ordered the traitor to be shot.

228. The infinitive is used after prepositions, where in English the gerund is employed—the Dano-Norwegian language having no gerund; any preposition may govern the infinitive; Ex. *De gjorde ret i at sige det til ham* you did right in telling it to him; *jeg er kommen hid for at tale med Dem* I came here to speak to you; *jeg reiste til Markedet for at kjöbe en Hest* I went to the fair to buy a horse; *efter at have sagt Farvel gik han sin Vei* (after) having bidden farewell he went away; *det gaar langsomt med at faa samlet Pengene* there is tardy progress in collecting the money; *for at tjene Penge ofrede han sit gode Navn og Rygte* in order to make money he sacrificed his good name and reputation.

229. The present participle cannot be used periphrastically with the verb *at være*, to be, as in English. I was just thinking about what to do must be rendered: *jeg tænkte netop paa, hvad der var at gjöre.* "The widow was mending the clothes of her youngest son," must be rendered: *Enken holdt paa at gjöre istand sin yngste Söns Klæder.* Note the use of the participle in the following sentences: *han kom löbende* he came running; *han blev staaende* he remained standing or: he came to a stand still. A second verb connected with such a participle by *og*, and, is not put in participial form but in the infinitive: *han blev staaende* *midt paa Gulvet og glo* he remained standing in the middle of the floor, staring.

Colloquially and vulgarly a present participle in–s is sometimes formed without any passive signification. *Han kom gaaendes* he came walking. Or with signification of what is to be done (cfr. lat. gerundive). *Kongen er ventendes* the king is to be expected. Sometimes, especially in advertisements, the active participle is used with signification of passive: *mit iboende Hus* the house I live in; *et byggende Skib* a ship that is being built (cfr. the Engl. expression: efforts are making.)

NOTE. Expressions like the following: "Having made the necessary preparations Mr. Jones at once started on his voyage" can not in Dano-Norwegian be rendered by means of a participle: *efter at have fuldendt sine Forberedelser tiltraadte han straks sin Reise.*

230. The past participle in compound tenses formed by means of the auxiliary *have* is indeclinable; the past participle in compound tenses formed by means of the auxiliary *være* follows the gender and number of the subject in so far as it is susceptible to the corresponding inflection: *Han er gaaet* he is gone; *de er (e) gaaede* they are gone; *jeg erkommen* I have come; *vi er(e) komne* we have come; *jeg er bleven* (colloquially N. *blit*) *meget syg* I have grown very ill; *vi er(e) blevne forviste fra vort Fædreland* we have been expelled from our native country (colloquially in Norway: *vi er blit* (or *blet*) *forvist*.)

The past participle is often used as an adjective and may in that capacity also be employed as a substantive; the participle of intransitive verbs may then have an active signification: *en bortreist Mand* a man who has departed; *et fortabt Faar* a lost sheep.

THE PASSIVE VOICE.

231. As is seen from the paradigm § 208 the passive may be formed through all its tenses by means of the auxiliary *blive*; but in the present, imperfect and infinitive (accordingly also in the future) there also occurs another form ending in—*es*.

NOTE 1. The passive in–*es* is a formation peculiar to the Scandinavian group of the Teutonic languages. It was originally a medial or reflexive formation, the terminal *s* being derived from original–*sk* (representing the reflexive pronoun O. N. *sik*.) This original reflexive signification is retained in many words; *ængstes—ængste sig* to be alarmed; *harmes, vredes* to get angry; *undres–undre sig* to wonder, etc.

NOTE 2. The form in -*s* is sometimes used in a reciprocal signification: *vi sees igjen* we are going to see each other (*i. e.* to meet) again; *mödes* to meet; *træffes* to meet; *slaas* to fight; *kappes* to vie with each other; *kives* to quarrel; *strides* to dispute; *næbbes* to bill; *mundhugges* to quarrel; *enes* to agree, etc.

Sometimes the verb is used this way in connection with a preposition where the pronoun contained in the reflexive verb must be taken to be governed by the preposition; Ex. *at tales ved* to speak with each other (in Norway they still say dialectically *tale ved en*, generally *tale med en*); the preposition is used adverbially in *skilles ad* to separate, *fölges ad* to go to-gether; *hjælpes ad* to assist each other.

232. Some verbs which only occur in passive form and some others, that have both an active and a passive form, but with an entirely different meaning, are called d e p o n e n t v e r b s ; Ex. *lykkes* to succeed; *blues* to be ashamed; *længes* to long; *ældes* to grow old; *mindes* to remember (but *minde* to remind), *findes* to exist (but *finde* to find), *gives* to exist (G. *es giebt'* from *give* to give). These deponent verbs, and to this class are also counted many of the above mentioned reciprocal verbs, form a deponent participle; Ex. *det har lykkedes* (also *lykkets, lyktes*) *mig* I have succeeded in—; jeg *har længtes* I have been longing. But this form is not very much in use and is generally avoided, whenever possible.

233. The two passive forms may in some instances be used promiscuously. But the form in–*s* is much more common than the other one, especially in the present tense and the infinitive (after the verbs *skal, maa, bör* etc.) The imperfect of the compound form occurs much more frequently than the present.

The compound form (*blive rost* to be praised) signifies the complete passivity, where all action on the part of the subject is wholly excluded, hence it is used to denote the single recorded fact, while the form in–*s* is used to denote a common condition or general rule.

The imperfect in–*s* is not used of strong verbs with radical vowel *a* in imperf. followed by two or more consonants: (not *sanges* but) *blev sungen* was sung; (not *tvanges* but) *blev tvungen* was forced; (not *drakkes* but) *blev drukket* was drunk; (not *stjales* but) *blev stjaalen* was stolen; note: *fandtes* existed, but *blev funden* was found; *gaves* existed, but *blev given* was given.

In the future passive the form *jeg vil roses* cannot be used except to denote: I wish to be praised. The simple future is either: *jeg skal roses* or *jeg skal* or *vil blive rost*; Ex. *vilde hun inviteres*? did she wish to be invited (E. Brandes: En Politiker.) The reason is that the verb *vil* and the ending in–*s* both imply so much activity, that they combined cannot possibly convey a passive meaning.

REFLEXIVE AND IMPERSONAL VERBS.

234. R e f l e x i v e verbs are those that always have as their object a pronoun denoting the same person as the subject; Ex. *at skamme sig* to feel ashamed; *jeg skammer mig* I feel ashamed, *han skammer sig, vi skamme(r) os, I skamme(r) eder, de skamme(r) sig.*

Transitive verbs may be used reflexively; Ex. *at slaa sig* to hurt one's self (*at slaa* to beat); *at vise sig* to appear (*at vise* to show).

NOTE. *At hænde, at hænde sig, at hændes* all indicate : to happen : *da hændte det, at—, du hændtes det, at—, da hændte det sig, at—*then it happened that.

235. I m p e r s o n a l verbs are those that have only the demonstrative pronoun neut. *det* as subject; Ex. *det regner* it rains; *det sner* it snows, etc. ; *det dages* it dawns; *det vaares* spring comes; or there may be a definite subject of the 3d person; Ex. *Forsöget mislykkedes* the attempt was unsuccessfull. *En Ulykke hændte* a misfortune happened (only the active *hænde* can be used in this manner, not *hændes* or *hænde sig*.)

Any passive form may be used impersonally; intransitive verbs cannot be used in passive, except impersonally. Such intransitive verbs used impersonally do not take the subject *det*, but in its stead the demonstrative adverb *der* is used; Ex. *der reises meget i Norge i Sommer* there is much travel going on in Norway this summer. In poetry *der* may be omitted: *nu tales jo lydt om, at Folket er vakt* now they talk so much about the people being aroused.

THE ADVERBS.

236. The neuter form of most adjectives can be used as an adverb: *snart* soon; *höit* high or highly; *smukt* nicely; *godt* well etc.

NOTE. Of adjectives ending in *-ig*, *-lig* in Norway the common gender form is used as adverbs but in Denmark the neuter: D. *oprigtigt*, N. *oprigtig* candidly; D. *ærligt*, N. *ærlig* honestly (in both cases pronounced oprigti, ærli).

Adverbs may furthermore be formed of adjectives (and partly of nouns) by the following endings:

1. —*lig*: *snarlig* soon; *nylig* recently; *storlig* greatly (of nouns: *öieblikkelig* instantly; *hovedsagelig* chiefly; *fængslig* only in connection with the verb *anholde*: *fængslig anholde* to arrest, derived from *fængsel* prison).

2. —*vis*, *heldigvis* happily; *lykkeligvis* happily; *tydeligvis* plainly (of nouns *delvis* partly; *parvis* in pairs; *skevis* by one spoonful).

3. —*e*: *bare* only; *ilde* ill; *vide* widely; *gjerne* willingly; D. *grumme* highly.

NOTE. To the adjective *god* good correspond the adverbs *godt* and *vel*. Sometimes both may be used promiscuously: *jeg ved det godt* and *jeg ved det vel* I know it well. In other cases one of them alone can be employed: *lev vel* live well (*i. e.* good bye); *sov godt* sleep well (but *sov vel og dröm behageligt* sleep well and have agreeable dreams); *vel* is also used by adjectives and adverbs in the meaning of rather: *det er vel meget af det gode* it is rather much of a good thing (not quite as strong as: *det er for meget*).

237. Adverbs which have the same form as the neuter (or in Norwegian in some cases the common) gender of the adjectives are susceptible of comparison:

snart soon *snarere* *snarest*
höit highly *höiere* *höiest* (or *höist*)

Ex. *jeg sidder höiest oppe i Træet* I am highest up in the tree; *jeg er höist ulykkelig* I am most unhappy.

Also some ending in —*e*:

længe long (time) *længere* or *længer* *længst*
(also: *langt* *længere* or *længer* *længst*)
ofte often far *oftere* *oftest*

The following adverbs have a different stem in comparative and superlative from that of the positive;

vel well *bedre* *bedst*
ilde badly *værre* *værst*
gjerne willingly *hellere* or *heller* rather *helst*

Jeg vil heller danse end synge I will rather dance than than sing (but it is rather a large house—*det er et temmelig stort Hus.*)

238. The adverbs are generally by grammarians divided according to their use in the sentence into demonstrative, relative, interrogative and indefinite, or according to their signification into adverbs of time, place, mode, degree etc. We shall here only mention some peculiarities in the formation and use of some adverbs:

bort away (to a place) *borte* away (in a place)
derhen thither *derhenne* there
hvorhen whither *hvorhenne* where
frem forth *fremme* in front
ind in (to a place) *inde* in (in a place).

hjem home	*hjemme* at home
ned down (to a place)	*nede* down (in a place)
op up (to a place)	*oppe* up (in a place)
ud out (to a place)	*ude* out (in a place)
siden since	*for lang Tid siden* long ago
saaledes } thus *saadan* }	*hvorledes* } how. *hvordan* }

saadan and *hvordan* may also be used as adjectives; *saaledes* and *hvorledes* only as adverbs.

The affirmative adverb *ja* is used in answer to a positive query, *jo* to a negative. *Har Hr. Persen været her idag? Ja.* Has Mr. P. been here to-day? Yes. *Har ikke Hr. Persen været her idag?* Has not Mr. P. been here to-day? *Jo* Yes.

NOTE. The more the better is in D.-N. *jo mere desto* (or *des*) *bedre; jo mere vi gik, desto længere syntes vi at være borte fra vort Maal* the more we walked along the farther we seemed to be from our destination; colloquially there may also be said *jo mere jo bedre* in the same meaning.

239. About the demonstrative local adverb *der* and the interrog.–rel. local adv. *hvor* can be noticed that they are used in many compounds without any local signification representing the dem. pronoun neuter *det* and the relative-interr. *hvilket; derpaa* thereupon; *derefter* thereafter; *derfor* therefore; *hvorefter* after which; *hvorfor* why.

THE PREPOSITIONS.

240. The prepositions do not in the language as it is to-day govern any case, except that in the pronouns which have separate forms for the subjective and objective case, the latter always follows the preposition: *hos mig* with me; *til ham* to him; *der er intet ondt i ham* there is nothing bad about him; *i Huset* in the house; *paa Gaden* in the street.

NOTE. In some phrases the ancient cases have been retained as governed by prepositions; the nouns either end in *-e* or *-s*, the latter being the genitive singular, the former representing an original genitive plural (in the ancient language ending in *-a*) or dative singular (in the ancient language ending in *-i*); in some cases the preposition and the noun governed by it are written together in one word, so as to show that the whole expression now is considered as an adverb; Ex.: *ihænde* (dat sing) at hand; *ilive* alive; *itide* in due, good time, *igjære* in progress; *isinde* in mind; (*gaa en*) *tilhaande* to assist somebody (literally go him to the hands; gen. pl.); *tillands* on shore; *tilsös* (N. *tilsjös*) at sea; *tilvands* at sea; *tilskibs* on a ship; *tilbords* at table (but *tilhest* on horseback); *have en tilbedste* to make fun of one; *have noget tilgode* to have something coming due; *til Thinge* at the court session.

241. In relative sentences introduced by *som* the preposition comes at the end of the sentence; Ex. *min Ven, som jeg ikke paa længe har hört fra, er död* my friend, from whom I have not had any news for a long time, has died; sometimes a preposition may be used adverbially at the end of the sentence: *en Hat med et sort Baand omkring* a hat with a black ribbon a r o u n d it; *Karl har faaet en stor Tavle at skrive paa* Charles has got a big slate to write on; *nu har han faaet sig en Vogn, han kan kjöre rundt i* now he has got a carriage in which to ride around.

242. As to the distinction between *i* in and *paa* on may be noticed that *paa* is always used in connection with the name of islands and in Norway with the names of certain (especially minor) towns; Ex. *paa Sjælland* in Zealand; *paa Bornholm* in B.; *paa Island* in Iceland (but *i England, i Irland*); *paa Moss* at Moss; *paa Kongsberg* at K.; *paa Fredrikshald* at F.; (but *i Fredriksstad, i Kristiania, i Drammen, i Skien, i Bergen, i Stavanger, i Trondhjem*). The use varies also with the names of different districts; *paa Hedemarken* in H.; *i Østerdalen* in Ø.

Af of; *fra* from: *En af os* one of our number; *en Mand fra Byen* a man from the city; *Johnsen er fra Aarhus* J. is from A.; *Jeg reiste fra Kristiania til Bergen* I went from Chr. to B. A rich merchant of Copenhagen (is in D.-N.) *en rig Kjöbmand i Köbenhavn*, but a r. m. of this city *en rig Kjöbmand her af Byen*; *Hekla af Kjöbenhavn* H. of Copenhagen.

NOTE. The following prepositional phrases are used as prepositions: *istedenfor* (also written *i Steden for, i Stedet for*) instead of; *paa Grund af* on account of; *i Anledning af* on the occasion of; *i Kraft af* in virtue of; *ved Hjælp af* by means of.

CONJUNCTIONS.

243. The conjunctions are divided into co-ordinating and sub-ordinating; both these classes are again divided according to their signification into several subdivisions.

The grammarians mostly enumerate the conjunctions belonging to the several classes, but we shall here only mention those of special importance or about the use of which there is anything to remark.

A. Co-ordinating:

og and; *baade—og* both —and; in the same meaning: *saa vel—som* as well—as: *jeg saavel som du* or *saavel jeg som du* I as well as you; *dels—dels* partly—partly; *snart—snart* now—now; *han er snart kold, (og) snart varm* now he feels cold, now warm; *eller* or; *enten—eller* either—or; *hverken—eller* neither—nor; *thi* for; *men* but.

B. Subordinating:

da when, as; indicates both time and cause; *da han kom, var jeg allerede gaaet* when he came I was already gone; *da han har forbrudt sig, maa han straffes* as he has offended, he must be punished; *siden* since (temp. and causal); *forsaavidt (som)* in so far as; *hvis, dersom, om* if; *hvis ikke, medmindre* if not, unless; *skjönt, endskjönt, omendskjönt* although, admit something actually existing; *om end, selv om* though, even if, admit something supposed; *at* that: *jeg ved at De har været her* I know that you have been here; *at* may also be omitted: *jeg ved De har været her* I know you have been here; *forat* in order that. Ex.: *Kjöbmanden sendte sin Sön til Udlandet, forat han skulde lære Sprog* the merchant sent his son abroad in order that he should learn languages (also *forat lære Sprog* to study languages, see §228;) *jeg lægger op Penge, forat jeg kan nyde en sorgfri Alderdom* I lay money by in order to be able to enjoy a comfortable old age (or *for at kunne nyde en sorgfri Alderdom*); *jeg gav ham en Krone, forat han skulde give den til Tiggeren* I gave him a Crown to give to the beggar. The infinitive construction is regularly employed when the infinitive and the predicate verb have the same subject, and often when the subject of the infinitive is the objeet of the predicate verb; in other cases *forat* must be used with a sentence. (Obs. *for* with an infinitive *at* written separately: *for at*, while the conjunction is written as one word: *forat*); *forat ikke* (or after a verb signifying f e a r *forat*) lest; Ex. *Borgerne brændte Byen, forat den ikke skulde falde i Fiendens Hænder* the citizens burned the town, lest it should fall into the hands of the enemies; *Borgerne var bange fo*r, *at Byen skulde falde i Fiendernes Hænder* the citizens were afraid, lest the town should fall into the hands of the enemies; *saa at* so as to; Ex. *mine Reisefæller har forladt mig, saa at* (or only: *saa) jeg er nu ganske alene* my traveling companions have left me, so I am now perfectly alone; *Stedet er saa öde, at det er formeligt uhyggeligt* the place is so desolate that it is (or: as to be) dismal; *end* than; *han er större end jeg* he is larger than I (colloquially is said: *han er större end mig* he is larger than me—but only: *Hr. Persen har et större Hus end jeg* Mr. P. has a larger house than I); *dette er noget ganske andet, end hvad vi saa igaar* this is something quite different from what we saw yesterday.

INTERJECTIONS.

244. The interjections proper are natural sounds, hardly to be counted among the forms of articulate speech, consequently they are beyond the domain of grammar. We shall here only mention that the D.-N. equivalents of h a l l o o *hallo, halloi, hei* are n o t used as a salute; as regards interjectional phrases may be mentioned that the equivalents of h o w d o y o u d o *hvorledes har De det, hvorledes staar det til med Dem* are only used when it is really intended to ask about somebody's health. As a simple greeting is employed: *god Dag* good day! (*god Morgen, god Aften*, good morning, good evening, and when leaving *god Nat* good night). *Om Forladelse!* beg your pardon! *undskyld!* excuse me; *tör jeg spörge?* if I may ask? *Tak!* thanks, thank you. *Mange Tak, Tusind Tak* many thanks, a thousand thanks! *ingen Aarsag!* don't mention it, not at all; *værsgo!* (i. e. *vær saa god*, in which form it is written) if you please, please (when fetching or offering somebody something); *vær saa venlig* (N. *vær saa snil*) *at gjöre det for mig* please do it for me; *strax paa Öieblikket* at once, right away.

The English Sir in yes, sir; no, sir is not translated unless when speaking to a superior or a person of rank in which case the title is added: *ja, Hr. Kaptain* (N. *Kaptein*) yes, Captain; *nei, Hr. General* no, General. But m a'm, madam, is translated *Frue* (Mrs.) or *Fröken* (Miss) according to circumstances: *Nei, Fröken, det tror jeg ikke* no ma'm, I don't think so; *Nei, Frue, det har jeg aldrig sagt* no, ma'm; that I have never said.

THE ORDER OF THE WORDS IN THE SENTENCE.

245. In a sentence consisting only of subject and predicate the former is placed before the latter; *Manden kommer* the man comes; if the position is inverted, then the sentence assumes an interrogative meaning: *Kommer Manden?* does the man come? If the predicate has an object the order of the words is as follows: subj.—pred.—obj.; *Hesten bar Rytteren* the horse carried the rider. The indirect object is placed before the direct object: *Fader gav Johan Bogen* father gave John the book; in interrogative sentences only the position of subj. and predicate is inverted: *Gav Fader Johan Bogen?* did father give J. the book. An adjective as attribute is placed before the noun: *en stor Hund, den store Hund* a big dog, the big dog; so also a genitive before the noun governing it: *Mandens Hus* the man's house; *Ciceros Taler* the speeches of Cicero. An adverb determining an adjective or other adverb is placed before the word which it determines, but an adverb determining a verb is placed after it: *en meget smuk Mand* a very handsome man; *Karl gik meget hurtigt* Charles walked very fast.

NOTE. The personal pronouns and the demonstrative plural *de* having retained their objective form (*mig, dig,* etc.) may in dependent function exchange position with the subject without causing ambiguity: *Ham saa jeg* him I saw; *hende gav jeg mine bedste Tanker* to her I gave my best thoughts. When it is desired to emphasize any certain part of the sentence it may be given the first place in the sentence ; in that case the subject always follows after the predicate: *Johan gav han en Bog og Marie en nydelig Dukke* he gave Johnny a book, but Mary a beautiful doll.

246. Interrogative and relative words (pronouns, adverbs and particles) and all conjunctions always take the first place. In interrogative sentences the predicate always precedes the subject, if the latter is not itself the interrogative word: *hvad har du der?* What have you got there? if the predicate is a compound form of the verb the subject is placed immediately after the auxiliary: *hvor har du været?* Where have you been.

In relative sentences the subject follows immediately after the relative word, if this latter is not itself subject: *det Hus, som du har kjöbt er meget daarligt* the house, which you have bought is very poor. *Overalt, hvor han har været, har han gjort sig forhadt* wherever he has been he has made himself disliked.

After conjunctions the words as a rule follow in the ordinary succession: *naar jeg kommer til Byen skal jeg kjöbe mig nye Klæder* when I go to town I shall buy myself a new suit of clothes.

NOTE 1. The inverted position of interrogative sentences is sometimes used in conditional propositions when the conjunction is omitted: *kommer jeg til Byen, skal jeg hilse din Moder fra dig* or *hvis jeg kommer til Byen, skal* etc. if I come to town I shall bring your mother your greetings.

NOTE 2. Antiquated and chiefly used in official and commercial correspondence is the custom of inverting the subject and predicate after *og* and; Ex. *denne Feiltagelse var meget uheldig, og formener Departementet, at den burde have været undgaaet* this error was very unpleasant and the Department believes that it ought to have been avoided.

247. As to p u n c t u a t i o n the D. N. language follows about the same rules as the English, excepting that comma is always used between the principal and the subordinate proposition. Comma is also used before independent propositions introduced by *og* and, and before single words connected by *men* but. Before complete sentences introduced by *men* but, semicolon is used. *Sig mig, hvad du har gjort!* Tell me what you have done! *Den Ring, som jeg havde paa Fingeren, er kommet bort* the ring I had on the finger has been lost. *Min Söster fortalte, at hendes Bog, som hun havde lagt fra sig paa Bordet for en Time siden, var forsvunden, da hun kom tilbage til Værelset:* My sister told me that her book which she had left on the table an hour ago had disappeared, when she returned to the room.

EXERCISES.

at være to be
Jeg, du, (De), han er I am etc.
vi, I, de er(e) we are etc.
   (see § 221).
Jeg, du, (De), han var I was etc.
vi, I, de var(e) we were etc.

at have to have.
Jeg, de, (De), han har I have etc.
vi, I, de have we have etc.
Jeg, du, (De), han havde I had etc.
vi, I, de havde I had etc.

Kat cat;	*Horn* (n.) horn;	*Ræv* fox;
Hus (n.) house;	*Maane* moon;	*Hale* tail;
Hest horse;	*Ko* cow;	*stor* big;
Næse nose;	*Haar* (n.) hair;	*Mand* man;
Bonde farmer;	*long* lang	*Mark* field.

(§§ 150—155) Katten har Næse, og (*and*) Maanen har Horn, og Ræven har Haar paa (*on*) Halen. Katten har en lang Hale. Koen har Horn, men (*but*) Hesten har ikke (*not*). Bonden har en Hest og en Ko. Den lange Næse, som (*which*) Manden har, forskjønner (*beautifies*) ham (*him*)ikke. Maanen skinnede (*shone*) paa det store Hus. I Huset var der en Kat med (*with*) lang Hale.

The horse and the cow were in the house, but the man was in the field. He was looking at (*saa paa*) the moon. The man has a long nose, but no (*ikke noget*) hair on his (use def. art.) head (*Hoved*, pron. hode). The house is large. The moon shines on the large house and on the field, on the horse, on the cow and on the cat.

(§ 161.) I Arken var ikke et Ark Papir (*paper*) at faa (*to be had*). Men der var en Buk, som gjorde (*made*) et dybt (*low*) Buk for Noa, da (*when*) han (*he*) med sit (*his*) Følge forlod (*left*) Arken. Fyren havde fundet (*found*) sig et Leie i Fyret, men han betalte (*paid*) ingen (*no*) Leie. Barnet (*child*) har en Værge, men Soldaten (*soldier*) har et Værge.

This (*denne*) draught is a special (*eiendommeligt*) feature of this (*dette*) house. The fellow had the choice (*Valget*) between (*mellem*) the rice and the rod. A soldier without (*uden*) weapon is a miserable (*elendig*) fellow. The father (*fader*) is [the] guardian of (*for*) his child.

(§ 163.) Form the possessive of the following words, with and without the article:

Slot (n.) castle.   *Tag* (n.) roof.   *Farve* color.
Bog book.   *Hjærte* heart.   *Ven* friend.
Bind (n.) cover.   *Fiende* enemy.

Et Tags, Tagets. En Farves, Farvens. Bogens. Mit (*my*) Hjærtes, Hjærtets. En Vens, Vennens. Min (*my*) Vens Bog har et rødt (*red*) Bind. Bogens Bind er rødt. Bindets Farve er rød. Den røde Farve er Hjærtets Farve. Farven paa (NB .) Bogens Bind er rød. Vær (*be*) din (*your*) Vens Ven.

The roof of the castle. The color of the roof of the castle is red. Be not the friend of your enemy's friend. My friend's enemy is my (*min*) enemy.

(§ 168.) Form the plural of the following words with and without the article:

Have garden.	*Lampe* lamp.	*Stue* parlor.
Kirke church.	*Skuffe* drawer.	*Værelse* room.
Muffe muff.	*By* city.	*Sö* (N. *Sjö*) sea.
Mark field.	*Skaal* bowl.	*Sön* son.
Ven.		*Blomst* flower.

Min Vens Sønner er(e) min Søns Venner. Min Ven har ingen (*no*) Fiender. Mit Hus har to (*two*) Stuer og fire (*four*) smaa (*small*) Værelser. Paa Markerne rundt (*around*) Byen er der mange (*many*) Blomster. Brooklyn har mange Kirker. Kirkernes Tal (*number*) er stort (*large*).

The friends of my son are sons of my friend. The enemies of my (*mine*) friends are not my friends. My house has two (*to*) gardens. In (*i*) the gardens are (*er der*) many flowers.

(§ 169.) Form the plural of the following words:

Dör door	*Sten* stone	*Kniv* knife.
Dag day	*Dal* valley	*Elv* river.
Fjeld mountain	*Bæk* brook	*Fjord*.
Kat cat	*Snedker* joiner	*Amerikaner* American.
Skomager shoemaker		*Skrædder* tailor.

Dette Værelse har to Døre. I Norge er der mange Bække, fulde (*full*) af Ørret (*trout*). Elve og Bække, Fjorde og Sjøer, Fjelde og Dale er Norge fuldt (*full*) af. Mine Brødre har mange Venner, og mine Søstre har mange Veninder. Fædre og Sønner.

These (*disse*) mountains and valleys with (*med*) their (D. *deres*, N. *sine*) rivers and brooks are rather (*temmelig*) monotonous (*ensformige*). Shoemakers and tailors are useful (*nyttige*) members (*Medlemmer*) of society (*Samfundet*).

(§§ 170—171). Decline the following neuter words: *Flag* flag; *Ben* bone, leg; pl. also feet; *Aar* year; *Dæk* deck. *Væddelöb* horse race.

Udstillingsbygningen (*the exposition building*) var dekoreret (*decorated*) med alle Nationers Flag. Mine Ben er(e) ømme (*sore*). Mine Forældre og Søskende have (N. har) mange Penge, men jeg har ingen. Min Vens Klæder er(e) af Klæde (*broadcloth*); men mine er(e) af Vadmel (*russet*). For mange Aar siden (*for siden* ago) havde jeg ogsaa mange Penge. Denne Mand er seks (*six*) Fod høi (*tall*).

The ship has two decks. The distance (*Afstand*) between (*mellem*) the decks is eight (*otte*) feet. Have you money, then you have (*saa har du*) food (*Mad*) and clothes.

(§§ 172—177.) Decline the following adjectives: *stor* big; *smuk* nice; *tam* tame, domesticated; *kostbar* expensive; *billig* cheap; *engelsk* English; *fransk* French; *glat* smooth; *öm* tender, sore; *barsk* severe, stern; *haard* hard; *varm* warm; *sund* healthy; *vanskelig* difficult; *simpel* simple; *kjölig* cool; *lydig* obedient.—

fölges ad go together.

Hesten, Hunden, Koen og Katten er tamme Dyr (*animals*). Smukke Klæder er(e) i Regelen (*as a rule*) kostbare; det billige (*what is cheap*) er sjelden (*seldom*) smukt. Et barskt Væsen (*manner*) og et ømt Hjerte følges ofte (*often*) ad, og det gjør ogsaa (*and so do*) et glat Ansigt og et haardt Hjerte.

The big city has many nice and expensive houses. A tame lion (*Löve*) is like (*som*) a big cat. Cheap and healthy residences (*Boliger*) are difficult to get (*skaffe*) in a big city. The cool night is very refreshing (*forfriskende*) after (*efter*) the warm day. A nice child (*Barn*, n.) ought always to (*burde altid*) be obedient.

(§§ 178—182). Decline the following adjectives:

sagte soft; *blaa*, *tro*, *fri*,
egen, *megen*, *afsides*, *nymodens*.

Den frie Mand og den frie Kvinde (*woman*) blev proklameret (*were proclaimed*) for alle Vinde (*winds*). Min egen Stue. Kongens eget Slot. Det ham (*him*) egne Væsen.

New-fangled ideas. Out-of-the-way towns. This man's eyes (*Öine*) are blue. A nice suit (*Sæt*) of clothes made (*syet*) of blue cloth.

(§§ 183—189). Compare the following adjectives:
kold cold; *söd* sweet; *blöd* soft;
venlig friendly; *from* pious; *ung*;
ond; *gammel*.

Min Broder er yngre end jeg, men jeg har et venligere Væsen. Det største Hus er ikke altid (*always*) det smukkeste. De ældste Børn er(e) de værste. Det nederste Trin (*step*) var ganske glat (*slippery*). Hr. Jensen er lærdere end Hr. Kristensen. Verdens (*in the world*) største Mand er ikke netop (*exactly*) den, som (*who*) veier (*weighs*) mest. Den yngste af de to Brødre er den smukkeste.

My father has the largest house in the block (*Kvartalet*) It has more windows (*Vinduer*) than (*end*) the other houses. The younger girl (*Pige*) is the handsomer. [N.B. Use the superlative in D N. in this case!]

(§§ 190—194). Har du min Bog? Nei, men jeg saa (*saw*) den (*it*) nu nylig (*just now*). Hvor (*where*) var den?

Den var paa Bordet i mit Værelse. Jeg har ikke lagt (*placed*) den der (*there*). Nei, din Moder lagde (*placed*) den der. Saa du hende gjøre (*do*) det (*it*)! Nei, men hun har selv (§196) fortalt (*told*) mig det. Min Broder fortalte (*told*) mig ogsaa (*also*), at (*that*) han havde seet (*seen*) den der. Den Den unge Mand har nylig mistet (*lost*) his Søn.

I have a nice little horse; have you seen it? My father gave (*gav*) it 'o me, and I thanked (*takkede*) him. Does (*kan*) your brother ride? No, he does not ride; but my sister does. She rides better than I do myself (§ 196). Once (*engang*) she lost (*mistede*) (§ 245 note) her hat while riding horseback (*mens hun var ude og red*). My parents (*Forældre*) have lost five (*fem*) of their [N B. different in Danish and in Norwegian] children.

(§§195—198.) Hvem er denne Mand med den lange Næse? Det er en Landstryger (*tramp*), som sælger (*sells*) Bliktøi (*tinware*). Undertiden (*sometimes*) stjæler (*steals*) han lidt fra saadanne Folk (*people*), som ikke holder (*keep*) deres (D., sine N.) Døre lukkede (*closed*). Hvor sover (*sleeps*) han? Hvem giver (*gives*) ham Mad (*food*)? Hvem faar (*get*) han Penge af? Han sover paa Marken, han spiser hvad han kan faa, og Penge har han ikke.

Who has got (*har*) my book? Which book do you mean (*mener*)? By (*af*) whom is the book? Whose book is it? Mine, of course (*naturligvis*). It is the book, that I placed on this table an hour ago.

(§§ 200, 201). Man siger (*say*), at nogen har været (*been*) her og ringet (*rung the bell*). Men da (*as*) ingen lukkede op (*opened the door*), gik (*went away*) de. Det kan ikke have været nogen af vore Venner. Nei, det var nogle fremmede (*strange*) Mennesker (*people*). Mangen Mand gaar (*goes*) hungrig (*hungry*) tilsengs (*to bed*), som man ikke vilde (*would*) tro (*believe*) det om (*about*).

They think that everybody can do this thing, but they are mistaken (*tage feil*). Nobody can learn (*lære*) a foreign (*fremmed*) language (*Sprog* n.) without persistent (*ihærdig*) work (*Arbeide* n.). Some called (*kaldte*) him a hero (*Helt*), others a humbug (*Humbugmager*). Many a heart is aching (*blöder*).

(§§ 202—205). Der er trehundrede og fem og seksti Dage i et Aar. Et Minut har seksti Sekunder (tresindtyve Sekunder). Min Søster er tolv Aar gammel. Tolv Gange tolv er hundrede og fire og fyrretyve (*or:* firti). For tyve Aar siden var jeg halvandet Aar gammel. En Centimeter er to Femtedels Tomme (*inch*). Han har sine Penge staaende (*standing*) paa (*at*) seks Procents Rente.

Some months (*Maaneder*) have 30 days and others have 31. One month, February, has only 28 days. The war (*Krigen*) lasted (*varede*) seven years. Seven times seven is 49. 20 years ago this big town was nothing but (*ikke andet end*) a little village (*Landsby*) My friend rises (*staar op*) at 6 in the morning (*om Morgenen*) and goes to bed (*gaar til sengs*) at 10 in the evening (*om Aftenen*).

(§ 208). Conjugate the following verbs:

bie to wait,   *hoppe* to jump,   *plante* to plant,
önske to wish,   *ofre* to sacrifice, spend,   *salve* to anoint,
raade to advise,   *vente* to wait,   *hakke* to peck.

Jeg har nu (*now*) ventet paa ham i en halv Time (*hour*), men nu kan jeg ikke bie længer. Jeg vil raade Dem til at vente en Stund (*while*) til (*more*). Nei, jeg har allerede (*already*) ofret for (*too*) megen Tid (*time*) paa ham. Jeg skulde have ventet en Stund til, hvis jeg ikke havde havt det saa travlt (*been so busy*). Se den lille Spurv (*sparrow*), som hopper udenfor Vinduet (*window*) og hakker i Vindueskarmen (*window frame*). Den venter paa at faa (*to get*) sin Frokost (*breakfast*).

EXERCISES. 139

Whom do you wish to see (*at tale med*) ? I wish to see your father? Please (*vær saa god at*) wait a while, he is not in (*hjemme*) just now (*netop i Öieblikket*) I can o ly (*bare*) wait 5 minutes. Cannot you spend any more time on him, he will be in (*kommer tilbage*) at 5 sharp (*paa Slaget fem*). What do you advise me to do ?

(§§ 210—211). Conjugate the following verbs:

tabe to lose,   *sluge* to devour,   *lede* to seek,
tale to speak,   *betale* to pay,   *laane* to borrow, to lend,
löse to loosen,   *sætte* to set,   *sætte sig* to sit down (§234),
               fölge to follow.

Fienderne tabte det første Slag (*battle*). Paa Slagmarken (*battlefield*) var mange Folk (*people*), som ledte efter deres (N. sine) Venner. Min Ven talte ikke til mig hele Aftenen. Det var, fordi (*because*) jeg har laant ham Penge, som han ikke kan betale tilbage (*back*). Han havde sat sig, dog (*yet*) stod han op (*got up*) og fulgte mig til Døren.

He spoke slowly (*langsomt*), as if (*som om*) he did not wish his audience (*Tilhörere*) to lose a single (*eneste*) syllable (*Stavelse*). An honest (*ærlig*) man pays back with interest (*Rente*) what he borrows Sit down and wait a little while, then I shall follow you to church (*Kirke*).

(§§ 213 and 214.) Skibet begyndte (*commenced*) at synke ti Minuter efter Sammenstødet (*collision*). Alle Passagererne (*passengers*) sprang til Baadene (*boats*), som var(e) bundne saa fast, at man maatte hugge dem løs (*loose*). Matroserne (*sailors*) havde drukket adskilligt (*considerably*) og vilde ikke slippe Passagerne ned i Baadene først. Tiggeren (*tramp*) bad først om Penge, men da de ingen gav him, kom (*came*) han igjen (*again*) om Aftenen og stjal, hvad de ikke vilde (*would*) give ham. Han havde seet Pengene ligge i en aaben Komodeskuffe (*bureau drawer*).

I found a dog, tied to the fence (*Gjærde*); it ran to-wards (*imod*) me as far (*langt*) as the chain (*Lænke*) would allow (*tillade*) it [to] It was very thirsty (*törst*), it had not drunk water (*Vand*) the whole day. I helped it to get out (*komme ud af*) the chain and gave it something to eat. While (*medens*) I was sitting (§ 229) by the roadside, I saw a man cutting (*skjære*, use inf.) grass in the field. Another man was helping nim.

(§§ 215—217). Da Musen (*mouse*) krøb frem (*forth*) af af sit Hul (*hole*), greb Katten den og vilde æde den. Men først vilde den lege (*play*) lidt men den. Den slap den, ligesom (*as*) om (*if*) den vilde lade (*allow*) den løbe (*run*), men saa (*then*) greb den den igjen og bed den ihjæl (*to death*). Det ryger fra Skorstenen (*chimney*), mens jeg røger min Cigar og nyder den. Medens du jagede Harer (*hares*) og skjød Ræve, jog (*chased*) jeg Fienden ud af Landet. Fienderne blev(e) slagne i tre Slag (*battles*), og mange af dem blev(e) tagne tilfangne (*made prisoners*).

I only (*kun*) obeyed [see § 245 in fine] your order (*Befaling*) when I chased the pigs (*Svinene*) out (*ud*) of the garden (*Have*) They had dug themselves an entrance (*Vei*) under the fence. They took the same way back again, and they pushed (*skjöv til*) each others in their efforts (translate i. th. e.: *idet de anstrængte sig for*) to get (*komme*) först ud.

(§§ 218—220). Naar (*when*) kom din Broder? Han kom for nogle Dage siden; nu skal han netop (*just*) gaa ud. Han gav mig en Velociped (*bicycle*), og Kristian fik et udmærket (*excellent*) Gevær (*gun*). Jeg laa og sov, da min Broder kom, men stod (*got*) straks (*at once*) op, da jeg hørte det ringe paa Klokken (*the bell*). Jeg kan ikke gjøre, hvad du beder mig om. Jo du skal og maa gjøre det. Tør De ikke gaa forbi Kirkegaarden (*cemetery*) om Natten? Jo, jeg er ikke bange (*afraid*) for Spøgelser (*ghosts*).

EXERCISES.

I know I ought to do it, but I dare not do it now. Yes, you must do it. What is your name, my friend? John is my Christian name (*Fornavn*) and Johnson is my family name (*Efternavn*). Did you sleep well last night (*inat*), Mr. Johnson? Yes, thank you. I slept very well and did not get up (get up: *staa op*) till (*før*) it (*Klokken*) was after (*over*) 8. Did you really (*virkelig*) stay in bed (*ligge*) as long as that. Yes, I have often stayed in bed longer than (*end*) that.

(§§ 234 to 235). Jeg skammer mig over at se, hvor (*how*) lidet jeg virkelig ved. Det hænder undertiden, (*sometimes*), at man ikke ved, hvad man skal gjøre. Det siges, at Kongen kommer (§ 222) hid (*here*) i Sommer (*this summer*). Det er blevet mig fortalt (*I have been told**), at ti Skibe forliste (*were lost*) i den frygtelige Orkan (*hurricane*), som blæste (*blew*) ifredags (*last Friday*).

I was told that I could come whenever I wanted to (*saa ofte jeg havde Lyst*). Don't you feel ashamed that you did not know this? No, I do not feel ashamed. You ought to do (*gjøre det*), at least (*i det mindste*). How did this thing happen?

(§§ 237—237.) Hr. Jones har besøgt (*visited*) os oftere i den senere Tid (*of late*), end han gjorde før (*formerly*). Ja, og han har været længer hver Gang. Hvor længe er det, siden du saa ham sidst (*the last time*)? Jeg saa ham for en Time siden. Vil De helst danse eller synge? Jeg vil gjerne begge Dele (*do both*). Hvor reiser De hen? Jeg reiser til Norge og tænker, jeg bliver to Maaneder borte (tænker, jeg bliver borte—*expect to be gone*). Har De ikke seet mine Handsker (*gloves*)? Jo, jeg har.

---

*) What is in the active the indirect object should not in D.-N. be made subject in passive. Some authors follow the English rule in that respect, but it is not considered good language.

How long do you expect to be gone? Four months. I would like to stay (*blive der*) longer, because (*fordi*) it is so long since I was there the last time. Why do you like better to dance than to sing? Because there is more fun (*Moro*) in it. Have you seen your father's hat? Yes, I have. Have not you seen your father's hat? Yes, I have

(§§ 240—242). Hvem har han hørt (*heard*) det af? Af mig kan han ikke have hørt det. Paa Island er der ingen Kjøreveie (*carriage roads*), saa der maa man overalt reise tilhest; men i Irland er der gode Veie. Min Broder Karl har været tilsøs i 25 Aar, saa det er nu paatide (*about time*), at han slaar sig ned (*settles*) tillands. Paa Grund af den tætte (*thick*) Taage (*fog*), kunde vort Skib ikke komme ind til Bryggen (*pier*).

Where do you come from? From Iceland. Have you been a long time in Iceland? Yes, I have been there quite (*temmelig*) long, and everywhere we had to travel around on horseback, because they had no roads there. By (*med*) which ship did you come from America? By the "Island" of Copenhagen. Have you been in any of the cities of Norway? Yes, I have been in Christiania and Bergen, and at Kongsberg and Fredriksstad.

(§ 243). "Dine Penge eller dit Liv" (*life*) er et haardt Valg (*choice*); men værre er det at miste baade Pengene og Livet. I Byens Udkant (*outskirts*) bor der mange fattige (*poor*), som hverken har Mad eller Klæder. Naar (*when*) du ikke vil høre, maa du føle (*must be made to feel*). Jeg maa straffe (*punish*) dig, forat du kan blive en brav (*good*) Mand. Min Søster har en smukkere Hat en du. Jeg har ingen bedre Ven end dig. Han er saa glad (*happy*), at han næsten ikke (*hardly*) kan lade være at (l. v. a.—*abstain from*) hoppe (*jump*) høit op i Veiret (*air*).

I give you this punishment (*Straf*) in order to improve (*forbedre*) your morals (*Sæder*). I make (*lader*) you study in order that you may be a useful (*nyttigt*) member (*Medlem*) of society (*Samfundet*). When (*naar*) I come here, I wish (*önsker*) to see everybody happy. When (*da**) I came home I saw many sad (*bedrövede*) faces (*Ansigter*). Neither my mother, nor my sister had such a nice hat as you had. A judgment (*Dom*) must either be right (*rigtig*) or wrong (*gal*), and it cannot be both right and wrong at the same time.

(§§ 245 –246). Hvem har De talt med (*seen*)? Jeg har talt med Deres Broder. Er det min ældste Broder, De har talt med? Hvor er min Hat? Deres Hat er her. Han gav en Tigger (*beggar*) sin nye Hat. Hvem gav han sin gamle Frak (*coat*). Træffer (*meet*) jeg dig her igjen, skal jeg lade (*have*) dig kaste (*throw*) ud af Vinduet.

Whom did you see? Where did you get (*faa*) that hat? I got it at the hatter's (*hos Hattemageren*), and I gave my old hat to a beggar. If I ever (*nogensinde*) see you again, I shall certainly (*visselig*) be most (*særdeles*) happy.

---

*) "When" referring to a single occurrence of the past is *da*, when referring to the future is *naar*. *Da*, besides time, indicates cause, *naar*, besides time, indicates condition.

Lessing's Minna von Barnhelm.

Based upon the text of Boxberger, in Joseph Kurschner's "Deutsche National-Literature." By SYLVESTER PRIMER, Prof. of Mod. Lang. in the University of Texas. 240 pages. Cloth. Price by mail, 70 cts. Introduction price, 60 cts.

LESSING may be said to have created the modern German stage, and his "Minna" is not only the first real German comedy but also the very best that the German literature has produced.

This edition contains: (1) Introduction. (2) (*a*) Biographical Sketch; (*b*) The development of the German drama and Lessing's influence upon it; (*c*) The position and influence of this work in German comedy; (*d*) Synopsis of the characters and their development in the play. (3) Text, followed by Notes and a Bibliography.

Prof. H. C. G. Brandt, *Hamilton College, in "Modern Language Notes":* Though edited again and again at home and abroad, it has never been so well edited before. (*June,* 1890.)

Prof. Waller Deering, *Vanderbilt Univ.:* Throughout the whole book Prof. Primer shows a fine appreciation of the student's needs. A perusal of the book leaves an impression of well-rounded completeness and scholarly thoroughness, which is indeed refreshing.

The Critic, *New York:* It is the best-provided text of this famous German comedy that we have. It is a monument in succinct form of patient research, helpful historical annotations, and practical insight into the needs of students. (*Sept.* 27, 1890.)

Literarisches Centralblatt, *Leipzig:* Ref. wüsste keine Ausgabe der "Minna" anzugeben, die so erschöpfend und dabei so anregend wäre wie diese. (*July* 26, 1890.)

Lessing's Nathan Der Weise.

Edited, with introduction and analytical and critical notes and a Bibliography by SYLVESTER PRIMER, *Professor of Teutonic Languages, University of Texas. Cloth. 338 pages. Introduction price, $1.00. By mail, $1.10.*

IF we except Goethe's *Faust*, no German poem has received so much special study as *Nathan der Weise*. It occupies the most prominent place in German Literature, after *Faust*, and is the most magnificent monument of Lessing's poetic genius. It deserves a place in the study of German, not only as a work of art, but also for the deep philosophical and scientific truths which it discusses.

The Introduction discusses amply the religious and philosophic back-ground of the drama, and gives a synopsis of the characters with their development in the play. The Notes aim to leave no real difficulty unexplained, and in the light of the best scholarship of to-day to interpret faithfully the thought of the author.

Schiller's Wilhelm Tell.

Edited, with Introduction and Notes, by R. W. DEERING, Ph.D., Professor of Germanic Languages, Western Reserve University, Cleveland, Ohio. Cloth. 280 pages. Introduction price, 60 cents. Mailing price, 70 cents.

THE present edition not only provides the play with adequate notes, which explain the linguistic difficulties and the historical and legendary allusions in the text, but also aims to increase the student's appreciation of the master's great work by enlisting his interest in the leading literary questions connected with it. The Introduction has thus included a critical analysis of the play, a concise account of the development of the Tell Legend and its relation to the real history of the Swiss struggle for liberty. A short Bibliography, including the best reference books, is added. This edition has a map.

James O. Griffin, *Asst. Prof. of German, Leland Stanford Univ.:* I am especially pleased with it, and find the introduction and notes most satisfactory. We shall use this edition in our classes.

A. R. Hohlfeld, *Prof. of German, Vanderbilt Univ.:* An excellent edition. The work of a thorough scholar and successful teacher. I shall introduce it.

Wilhelm Bernhardt, *Director of German in the High Schools, Washington, D.C.:* At last a worthy American edition. I shall use it with my classes.

J. T. Hatfield, *Prof. of German, Northwestern Univ.:* I am greatly gratified to find it so satisfactory. I introduce it at once.

Milton S. Churchill, *Prof. of Mod. Langs., Illinois Coll., Jacksonville:* I consider it a very excellent edition; in many particulars much superior to other school editions. We shall undoubtedly use it next year.

Edwin F. Norton, *Prof. of Mod. Langs., Olivet Coll., Mich.:* I am delighted with it. It suits me better than any other edition of this beautiful masterpiece. I shall introduce it.

Starr W. Cutting, *Asst. Prof. of German, Univ. of Chicago:* It is an excellent bit of editorial and typographical work, and will find a place in our next year's programme of courses.

Thomas Logie, *Prof. of Mod. Langs., Rutgers Coll.:* By far the best edition yet published.

Ottilie Herholz, *Prof. of German, Vassar Coll.:* I like it very much, and shall recommend it in our catalogue.

Dr. Theo. Neumann, *Inst. of Mod. Langs., Riverview Acad. Poughkeepsie, N.Y.:* I have looked forward to this edition and was sure it would be a fine one; now I must say that it is beyond my expectations, not only because of its elegant exterior, its beautiful print and the convenient arrangement of the whole, but by far more because of its careful and well chosen notes and the welcome introduction, which I have read with great delight.

F. A. Dauer, *Prof. of Mod. Langs., Geneva Nor. School, Ohio:* It will be permanently used here. The introduction shows most careful research and scholarship, and the notes are prepared with closest attention to the needs of the pupils.

Schiller's Maria Stuart.

Edited, with Introduction and Notes, by LEWIS A. RHOADES, Ph.D., Cornell University. Cloth. 254 pages. Introduction price, 60 cts. Mailing price, 70 cts.

THIS edition has been prepared with constant attention to the latest and best literary work in German on this great tragedy, and with a constant regard for the wants of students in school as well as college. The introduction contains a scholarly account of the genesis of the drama, and Schiller's historical sources, a critical discussion of the drama, the characters, the language and the meter. The notes explain fully all historical allusions, discuss grammatical peculiarities, and translate expressions which might not be made clear by an intelligent use of a German dictionary.

Scheffel's Ekkehard.

Abbreviated and edited with English notes by CARLA WENCKEBACH, Professor of the German Language and Literature, Wellesley College. Cloth. 241 pages. 70 cents.

THIS is one of the very greatest works in German fiction; a wonderfully vivid picture of life in the middle ages, full of interest, with many touches of humor, strong characterizations and attractive narrative. In order to bring it within suitable limits for use as a text-book, large omissions have been necessary, but this has been done so as to leave the narrative intact.

A. R. Hohlfield, *Prof. of German, Vanderbilt Univ.:* I am delighted with it. In this form it will be possible to use this masterpiece of German fiction for class work. The work seems to have been very skillfully done. I shall use it in our course.

C. W. Cabeen, *Prof. of German, Oberlin Coll.:* You have done American students of German a service in presenting this excellent edition. I shall take great pleasure in ordering it for class use.

J. T. Hatfield, *Prof. of German, Northwestern Univ.:* I am more than pleased with it. It is an admirable contribution to the study of German. I expect to introduce it next year.

H. H. Boyesen, *Prof. of German, Columbia Coll.:* I have examined it with pleasure. It is a very entertaining and serviceable text-book.

B. W. Wells, *Prof. of Mod. Langs., Univ. of the South:* The editor has preserved with great skill the spirit of the whole. I am convinced that the impression left on the mind of the students will be essentially the same as if the unabridged novel had been read; and this, considering the place Ekkehard occupies in German historical fiction, should suffice to commend it to all. I shall introduce the book immediately.

E. R. Ruggles, *Prof. of German, Dartmouth College,:* I have put it on the list of books to be used.

Schiller's Jungfrau von Orleans.

Edited, with an Introduction and Notes, by BENJ. W. WELLS, Ph.D. 248 pages. Cloth. Mailing price, 70 cents. Introduction price, 60 cents.

THIS edition has grown out of the needs of the editor's class room. *Die Jungfrau* is, on the whole, in his opinion, the best book with which to begin the study of the German classics.

The language is in general simple and clear, and offers few difficulties to students in their third or even their second term. But the drama has not hitherto been provided with a body of notes adequate to enable the student to enter fully into the spirit of the period and of the characters.

The Introduction contains an account of the genesis of the drama, its production on the stage, the MSS. and early editions, the metrical structure, and the historical sources, together with Schiller's additions and alterations. The notes are mainly grammatical and historical. At the end is an appendix on the Regimen of Verbs and the Subjunctive Mood as they appear in the drama. Also a map.

H. S. White, *Prof. of German, Cornell Univ.:* The commentary contains much that is valuable.

H. H. Boyesen, *Prof. of German Lang. and Lit., Columbia Coll., N. Y.:* It is a very creditable piece of work, the text being remarkably free from errors and the notes furnishing all supplementary information with commendable accuracy and conciseness.

E. R. Ruggles, *Prof. of Mod. Langs., Chandler Scientific Department, Dartmouth Coll.:* The Introduction and Biographical notices seem to me admirable and ought to be helpful and stimulating alike to instructor and student.

Geo. O. Curme, *Prof. of Mod. Langs., Cornell Coll., Ia.:* Am very much pleased with Die Jungfrau von Orleans and will use it next year and permanently establish it in our course. The edition is the best with which I am acquainted.

Thos. L. Angell, *Prof. of German, Bates Coll., Lewiston, Me.:* Your "Jungfrau von Orleans" introduced by me this year is an *excellent work.*

Carl F. Kolbe, A. M., *Prof. of Mod. Langs., Buchtel Coll., Ohio:* For seventeen years I have read the Jungfrau von Orleans, with my classes, considering this drama, the best with which to begin the study of the German Classics. Of all the editions which have come to my knowledge during this time, the one just now edited by Dr. Benj. W. Wells is unquestionably the best. I rejoice that such an edition has come at last to gladden both students and teachers.

Goethe's Hermann und Dorothea.

With introduction, commentary, bibliography and index to notes by WATERMANN T. HEWETT, M. A., Ph. D., Professor of the German Language and Literature in Cornell University. Cloth. 293 pages. Introduction price, 80 cts. Price by mail, 90 cents.

THE present edition is based on Goethe's final revision as contained in his collected works, which were being published at the time of his death. It gives also the readings of the earlier editions. The editor, in the preparation of this edition, has sought to lead from the study of this poem to a larger knowledge of the language, and especially to acquaintance with the thoughts of the author as illustrated in this and in his other writings.

Hence the notes have not been confined to brief grammatical explanations, but an effort has been made to interpret the poem from the poet himself. The sources of the poem, the author's language and the language of the time have been carefully studied. The history of the composition of the poem has been shown more fully by the recent publications of the Weimar Goethe Society, especially as contained in Goethe's Diary and Letters, and use has been made of these fresh materials.

It is believed that this edition will not only guide to an intelligent knowledge of the poem itself, but afford useful material for the critical study of the language and writings of the author.

Dr. G. Von Loeper, *the distinguished editor of Goethe's Works:* Professor Hewett's edition of *Hermann und Dorothea* has given me a very high opinion of the standard of literary studies in America. Professor Hewett in America, and M. Chuquet in France have attained the highest plane of excellence in those studies in the domain of classical German.

Prof. Edward Dowden, LL.D., *of the University of Dublin, and President of the English Goethe Society:* It seems to me admirable edited and very valuable both for student and teacher. I am exceedingly glad to have it among my Goethe books.

Dr. C. Ruland, *Director of the Goethe Museum in Weimar:* I have read your excellent introduction and looked through some of your notes and can only congratulate your countrymen on having Goethe's poem brought near to them in such a superior manner. Such editions do infinitely more good than a great deal of our dry-as-dust Goethe philology.

H. H. Boyesen, *Prof. Germanic Languages and Literature, Columbia College, New York:* I have already demonstrated my appreciation of Professor Hewett's excellent edition of *Hermann und Dorothea* by adopting it as a text-book in my classes. It is a beautiful book and exceedingly well done.

Goethe's Dichtung und Wahrheit.

First four Books. Edited especially for this Series, with Introduction and Notes, by C. A. BUCHHEIM, Professor of German, King's College, London, and editor of the Clarendon Press Series of German Classics. Cloth. 339 pages. Introduction price, $1.00. Price by mail, $1.10.

DICHTUNG und Wahrheit furnishes desirable reading for German classes, because it represents some of Goethe's most finished prose, and because of its interest as valuable autobiographical information. Three books of this work are recommended by the Commission of New England Colleges to be used in preparation for entrance on advanced requirements in German.

Goethe's Torquato Tasso.

Edited by CALVIN THOMAS, Professor of Germanic Languages and Literatures, Univ. of Michigan. 246 pages. Cloth. Price, by mail, 85 cents. Introduction price, 75 cents.

THAT "Torquato Tasso," one of Goethe's most important and characteristic works, has not hitherto been more generally read in American institutions of learning is doubtless due mainly to the fact that no satisfactory edition of the play was procurable. Professor Thomas has endeavored to make an edition befitting the present status of Goethe scholarship. The text is based upon a careful examination of all the extant sources of information. An ample Introduction describes the genesis of the drama, traces out its relation to its author's life, and discusses its ethical import. The notes are written not for the beginner in German who needs instruction upon the rudimentary facts of the language, but for students who are presumed to have acquired at least a budding interest in the higher aspects of German literature.

H. C. G. Brandt, *Prof. of German, Hamilton Coll.*: The introduction is excellent, and shows the thorough "Goethe Kenner." The notes are adapted to the needs of the grade of students that are able to undertake this masterpiece.

The editor addresses himself rather to the student of literature, the student of Goethe, than to the student of German language in and for itself. Considered from this point of view, the book must certainly be pronounced the best edition of a German Classic issued in this country.

Mod. Lang. Notes, *Baltimore, Md.:*

Goethe's Faust.

Erster und Zweiter Theil. Two volumes. Edited by CALVIN THOMAS, Professor of the Germanic Languages and Literatures, University of Michigan, Part I. Cloth. 435 pages. Introduction price, $1.12. By mail, $1.25.

THE distinctive feature of this edition of *Faust* — at least its most prominent distinctive feature — is that it presents the entire poem. Hitherto, although the First Part has been repeatedly edited, no complete edition of the work has been prepared for English-speaking students. The reason of this state of affairs is not hard to comprehend; it lies in the all too general neglect of the Second Part. Notwithstanding that this portion of the drama has been several times translated, and notwithstanding that individual scholars have long since felt its power and recognized its value, it has been slow in winning its way to the general favor that it deserves.

It is believed that American students of Goethe will now welcome a complete American edition of the poet's great work. The volumes are edited throughout on philological principles. The aim is, first, to throw light upon real difficulties of the text; at the same time the larger questions of criticism and interpretation are not neglected even if they must be treated briefly. [*Part II. in preparation.*

Kuno Francke, *Ass't. Prof. of German, Harvard Univ., in " The Nation:* It is not too much to say that of all the editions which thus far have appeared in this country or in England, this is by all odds the most scholarly and comprehensive. Its distinguishing feature is the spirit of directness and common sense that pervades it from beginning to end. It will mark an important step in the history of Goethe study in America.

M. D. Learned, *Ass't. Prof. of German, John Hopkins Univ.:* A vast stride forward in Faust study in America. This edition is marked by comprehensiveness of plan, wise selection of material, and clearness of statement.

A. H. Palmer, *Prof. of German Lang. and Lit., Yale Univ.:* Beyond question the best edition with English apparatus.

L. E. Horning, *Prof. of German, Victoria Univ., Toronto, Ont.:* It is as perfect as an edition of Faust can well be, and it is pleasant to find an editor who can be in full sympathy with his work without losing his balance.

Henry B. Longden, *Prof. of German, De Pauw Univ.:* I am delighted with it, and know of no edition comparable to it. I shall use it with my class.

A. R. Hohlfeld, *Prof. of German, Vanderbilt Univ.:* I am delighted with the edition, which is not only eminently useful, but also a credit to the country. I have already introduced it.

Literarisches Centralblatt, *Leipsic:* Wir wollen uns alles Bekritteln enthalten, angesichts eines Buches, das im Ganzen durchaus lobenswerth erscheint.

MODERN LANGUAGES.   BOOKS FOR BEGINNERS.

GERMAN. — *Sheldon's Short German Grammar.* (Price, 60 cents.)
 For those who have studied other languages and wish to learn to *read* German.

  Harris' German Lessons.) Price, 60 cents.)
 An Elementary Grammar, adapted for a short course or as introductory.

  Joynes-Meissner German Grammar.
 Part I., "Shorter German Grammar," 80 cents; complete Grammar, $1.12.

  Joynes' German Reader for Beginners. (Price, 90 cents.)
 An introduction to reading; with notes, vocabulary and English Exercises.

  Deutsch's Select German Reader. (Price, 90 cents.)
 With notes and vocabulary. May be used with or without a grammar.

  Boisen's Preparatory German Prose. (Price, 90 cents.)
 Excellent selections of prose with full suggestive notes.

  Van der Smissen's Grimm's Märchen and Der Taucher. (75 cents.)
 In Roman type. With full notes and vocabulary.

  Super's Andersen's Märchen. (Price, 70 cents.)
 Graded, as far as possible, and with notes and vocabulary.

  Faulhaber's One Year Course in German. (Price, 60 cents.)
 A brief synopsis of German Grammar, with reading exercises.

FRENCH. — *Edgren's Compendious French Grammar.*
 Part I., the *essentials* of French Grammar, 35 cents. Complete book, $1.12.

  Grandgent's Short French Grammar. (Price, 75 cents.)
 An Elementary Grammar, adapted for a short course or as introductory.

  Grandgent's Materials for French Composition. (12 cents each.)
 Pamphlets based on Super's Reader and other texts.

  Super's Preparatory French Reader. (Price, 80 cents.)
 Graded and interesting reading for school or college. With notes and vocabulary.

  Houghton's French by Reading. (Price, $1.12.)
 For home or school. Elementary grammar and reading.

  Lyon and de Larpent's French Translation Book. (Price, 60 cents.)
 A very easy Reader with English exercises for reproduction.

  Joynes' French Fairy Tales. (Price, 35 cents.)
 With notes, vocabulary and English exercises based on the text.

ITALIAN. — *Grandgent's Short Italian Grammar.* (Price, 80 cents.)
 All the Grammar needed for a short course.

  Grandgent's Italian Composition. (Price 60 cents.)

SPANISH. — *Edgren's Short Spanish Grammar.* (Price, 80 cents.)
 All the grammar needed for a short course.

  Todd's Cervantes' Don Quixote. (In press.)
 Twelve chapters with notes and vocabulary.

  Ybarra's Practical Method in Spanish. (Price, $1.20.)

D. C. HEATH & CO., Publishers,
BOSTON, NEW YORK, CHICAGO AND LONDON.

www.ingramcontent.com/pod-product-compliance
Lightning Source LLC
Chambersburg PA
CBHW030301170426
43202CB00009B/831